KT-872-575

Critical Guides to Spanish Texts

Critical Guides to Spanish Texts

EDITED BY J. E. VAREY AND A. D. DEYERMOND

BLASCO IBÁÑEZ

LA BARRACA

Richard A. Cardwell

Lecturer in Spanish in the University of Nottingham

Grant & Cutler Ltd *in association with*
Tamesis Books Ltd

© Grant & Cutler Ltd
1973
ISBN 0 900411 64 3
Printed in England at
The Compton Press Ltd
for
GRANT & CUTLER LTD
11 BUCKINGHAM STREET, LONDON, W.C.2.

Contents

Explanatory Note

All page references to the text of the novel are from *La barraca,* ed. G. J. G. Cheyne, 1st ed. (London, Harrap, 1964).

The figures in parentheses in italic type refer to the numbered items in the Bibliographical Note; the italic figure is followed by a page reference.

A. Grove Day and Edgar Knowlton, Jr. have recently published a study of the life and work of Blasco Ibáñez in English. *V.Blasco Ibáñez* (New York, Twayne, 1972), while not used in the preparation of this monograph, is recommended for its concise biography and the critical account of the major novels grouped under various periods. The final chapter considers the author's literary theories, quotes statements on the function of the novelist and examines the methods of composition, and, though general, is useful. There is also a selected critical bibliography and an index.

Quotations from E. Sebastià's *València en les novel·les de Blasco Ibáñez* (Valencia, 1966) and the extract from Zola's prologue to the second edition of *Thérèse Raquin* in chapter VII have been translated into English.

The following abbreviations have been employed :

CHA	*Cuadernos Hispanoamericanos*
HR	*Hispanic Review*
LNL	*Les Langues Néo-Latines*
MLR	*Modern Language Review*
PMLA	*Publications of the Modern Language Association of America*

1 La barraca *and the critics*

La barraca is concerned with a limited area of human experience. It is difficult for the modern reader to identify with this story of peasant struggles, set as it is in the Valencian *huerta* of the last century. Yet while the problems the author considers have now become a part of the social history of Spain, they nonetheless do not lack relevance for our own times. The novel is concerned with man's struggle for survival and his courageous attempts to come to terms with an apparently hopeless situation. The hero is faced with a dilemma. Coming from outside the rich agricultural region of Valencia, Batiste finds work only to discover that he is, in fact, betraying his fellow peasants. Yet he must work the forbidden lands and break the boycott. Victims of starvation and penury, the Borrull family cannot allow the sanctions of working-class solidarity to take priority over this last opportunity to find material prosperity. Batiste has no political allegiance, he identifies with no specific group of interests. He is the simple man who has the misfortune to be the victim of conflicting social interests.

However, *La barraca* is more than the story of social conflict. The themes and ideas of the novel are woven together in a complex, and often contradictory, statement concerning the human condition. What is of particular interest is the way in which the author draws on his acquaintance with various contemporary and topical scientific, sociological, political and philosophical theories. By means of these theories he is better able to resolve, or at least fully discuss, those problems that have engaged his interest. A second important factor is that the novel is set in a specific milieu, the *huerta*, and at a particular moment in history, the last decades of the nineteenth century. In order to understand fully the intention of the author, it is necessary to comment briefly on the political and social background to the period in which the novel was written.

S. Giner has concluded that in the nineteenth century "Spain was lagging well behind other Western countries in the dynamics of the stratificational system" and that it "deviated, in many respects, from the Northwestern European pattern". "This is clear", argues Giner, "in the absence of a nation-wide bourgeoisie, the persistence of semi-feudal distributions of land property, . . . the general dependence on a seasonal agricultural economy, . . . and the traditionalistic system of values held by most Spaniards at the time".* In the main, the rural proletariat lived in the environment most hostile to social change : small, isolated communities. The various possibilities for the amelioration of the conditions of the peasantry were frustrated by four principal factors : population pressures, *desamortización, caciquismo* and the Restoration political and economic system. By the mid-century social change began to quicken under the pressures of a large population expansion. Overseas emigration never quite eliminated these pressures in Spain. Indeed, its effect was to slow the breakdown of the semi-feudal structures of rural society and to maintain the *status quo*. Internal population movements, mainly from the arid central regions to the rich lands of the periphery, like Batiste's enforced migration, were soon to intensify class tensions by seriously disturbing the traditional ratio of workers to landowners and swelling the villages with seasonally unemployed. *Desamortización*, the sale of entailed property (usually ecclesiastical) under the liberal régimes of the 1840s, had two major effects. First, it marked the emergence of a landed bourgeoisie which briefly disturbed the semi-feudal stratification of class. More importantly, the poor peasants, who rented the disentailed lands from the bourgeoisie, derived little immediate benefit. In general the soil was unsuitable for individualistic, non-communal cultivation

*17, 13–14. The following also offer useful surveys of the period: P. Vilar, *Spain: A Brief History*, Oxford, 1967; W. C. Atkinson, *A History of Spain*, Harmondsworth, 1960; Carr, *16*; M. Buencasa, *El movimiento obrero español*, Barcelona, 1928; E. Hobsbawm, *Primitive Rebels*, Manchester, 1959; A. Jutglar, *Ideologías y clases en la España contemporánea*, Madrid, 1968; G. Brenan, *The Spanish Labyrinth*, Cambridge, 1943; J. B. Trend, *The Origins of Modern Spain*, Cambridge, 1934 and J. Díaz del Moral's excellent *Historia de las agitaciones campesinas*, Córdoba-Madrid, 1929.

without massive capital expenditure on irrigation. Exploitation of water shortage during droughts could, and did, ruin the peasant. Carr has argued that the restoration of the Monarchy in 1874 offered Spain social peace (*16*, 362). With the introduction of Cánovas' *turno pacífico* (an agreement between the two major political parties to alternate in office) and the development of the *cacique* system to ensure the desired result in each election, what was legally and formally a democratic monarchy became an oligarchy. In the countryside, which had never benefited from genuine agrarian reforms or capital investment, the *caciques* were able to consolidate a *de facto* feudal relationship with the peasants. The overall effect was to maintain the legitimate interests of property, deny any opportunity for a gradual process of political education, and foster corruption and political jobbery under the guise of concealed charity or offers of work. Patronage, says Carr, had always conditioned justice (*16*, 372). In the towns, municipal scandals were common. Blasco Ibáñez's own campaign over the *affaire Touchet* in Valencia, where the funds for public lighting were embezzled, is a case in point (*7*, 12). The *turno pacífico* implied ultimately the switch of personnel in administrative sinecures. Public service became private profit. While the civil servants and the well-to-do generally benefited, the peasant was usually deprived of amenities.

Throughout the 1870s and 80s the Restoration régimes could rely on the approval of the middle classes and the traditional support of the Church and nobility. "Until the 90s Spanish politicians could regard labour troubles . . . as questions of public order, . . . rather than as portents for the future" (*16*, 439). Yet the forces of radicalism were gaining ground. While the industrial population was never large, it provided a nucleus for working-class movements. In 1868, Fanelli, a disciple of Bakunin, arrived in Spain. In spite of ideological differences between the followers of Bakunin and authoritarian Marxists, by the 1880s workers' alliances, regional federations, associations and committees had been founded and congresses held. The dissemination of the classics of proletarian revolution, especially Kropotkin's *The Place of Anarchism in Socialist Evolution* (1886) and *The Conquest of Bread* (1906), did much to foster the growing organization of labour movements.† In Valencia, Blasco Ibáñez published, in cheap format, the works of Kropotkin, Zola, Renan, Gorki, Spencer and other 'revolutionary' writers. In that city, too, Blasco Ibáñez was a leading Republican figure, more inclined to Ruiz Zorrilla's philosophy of Republicanism imposed by force than the legitimist Castelar view that rejected methods of violence. Through his part in the founding of the Republican and separatist Liga Valenciana he became a notorious left-wing figure. For his part in the campaigns against the authorities over the colonial war in Cuba he became a wanted man. León Roca has described in some detail the turmoil of Blasco Ibáñez's life in Valencia in the 1880s and 90s (7 and *12*). Blasco demanded the right to public demonstration over the war issue. He bitterly criticised the reactionary declaration of military government in Valencia in the columns of his newspaper *El Pueblo*. In so doing he again ran foul of the authorities and yet another incarceration followed. Blasco Ibáñez had studied, and knew intimately, the agrarian problems of Valencia. Many of the questions outlined above are discussed in his *Historia de la revolución española* (3 vols, 1894). It is equally clear that they inform *La barraca*. For this reason both the author and his work attracted considerable attention from the outset. Given his radical views, criticism has tended to adopt clear-cut positions : either in support of or, more usually, in violent disagreement with his liberal attitudes. Indeed, a brief study of Blasco Ibáñez's reputation in Spain and the passions he has aroused will serve to show how hotly debated

---

†Blasco Ibáñez and his liberal contemporaries would probably have read the French versions of Kropotkin's work: *L'Anarchie dans l'évolution socialiste* and *La Conquête du pain* were both published in Paris in 1892. However, the major works were quickly available in Spanish, many published in Valencia. One of the most important translators was F. Salvochea who became the model for Blasco Ibáñez's anarchist heroes, especially in *La bodega*. See *Memorias de un revolucionario*, trad. de F. Salvochea, Madrid, 1895?; Salvochea also translated *El problema social* included in A. Lorenzo's *Biografía de Pedro Kropotkin*, Madrid, 1899 and *Campos, fábricas y talleres*, Madrid, 1899?. *La conquista del pan* was published before 1900, Azorín translated *Las prisiones* in 1897, *La anarquía* appeared in the late 1880s. See A. Lorenzo, *El proletariado militante*, Barcelona, Vol. I (1901), Vol. II (1923); J. J. Morato, *Historia de la sección española de la Internacional (1868-1874)*, Madrid, 1930; R. Pérez de la Dehesa, *El grupo "Germinal": una clave del 98*, Madrid, 1970; and Brenan (see note on p. 10 above).

were the issues he chose to discuss. The first assessment of *La barraca* is, for the age, surprisingly moderate.

Thirteen days after the final episode of *La barraca* appeared in the newspaper *El Pueblo* on 16 November 1898, the Republican anti-clerical *La Publicidad* published in Barcelona the first known critical essay on the novel. It is ironic that its author, Emilio Junoy, should immediately stumble on the essential meaning. Critics in Spain have in general failed to heed Junoy's moderate appraisal. The result is, as noted above, that their positions have tended to polarise : the one camp intemperately vicious, the other hotly partisan. It is only the modern reader who has the advantage of objective and more tranquil hindsight. Junoy's comments on *La barraca* echo the republicanism without radicalism characteristic of the articles which appeared in *La Publicidad*, so that he offers an interpretation that, as far as I know, has never been repeated. Contrary to what the detractors are to argue, Junoy asserts that the novel is not propagandistic :

> Es la negación rotunda de la política del odio que hoy prevalece en el espíritu del proletariado en su riña torpe y fatal con la democracia pública; es decirle noble y honradamente al pueblo que sufre y trabaja, cuán mal obra martirizando de hecho y de palabra.

Could it be that Blasco Ibáñez amid the uproar over the Cuban war, the head-on collision of *El Pueblo* with the Consejo de Guerra, the *affaire Touchet* (cf. p.11), the Republican campaigns, the founding of the Liga Valenciana, arrests, incarcerations, was able to detach himself sufficiently to write a novel that urged, not radical political action or even irreligious determinism, but a message of understanding and adjustment? Blasco Ibáñez may have been concerned in an experiment, as was Galdós, which was intended to demonstrate how a man can come to terms with reality.

Blasco Ibáñez's writings have always aroused an impassioned response. His work soon attracted praise from the liberal critics of *La Epoca* and *Vida Nueva*, and the keen interest of the French academics who contributed to the *Bulletin Hispanique*. But traditionalist and Monarchist critics reacted with scorn and invective. Rafael Conte, as late as 1967, the centenary of the novelist's birth, sombrely recorded that:

> Ni siquiera ese respetable plazo, estos cien años transcurridos, han posibilitado la aparición de la serenidad; . . . la figura de Blasco ejemplifica como pocas la dialéctica nacional.‡

Literary debate in the post-Romantic period has been constantly forced into familiar polemical patterns. The end of the century was to see the exaggeration of an ideological schism that had begun to appear in the 1830s.* It seemed "as if the participants could not properly understand the issues until they had perceived 'los dos bandos', which they do with a speed and certainty perplexing to the modern reader".† Such is the case with Blasco Ibáñez who has been vindicated as a liberal reformer, condemned as anti-religious and politically unorthodox, and has also been the object of well-meaning apology. E. Betoret Paris had, by 1969, become impatient with this lamentable state of affairs and took up the cudgels to deplore the general neglect and to point to Blasco Ibáñez as one of the few men in Spain in this century to show tolerance and integrity.‡‡ The literary historians writing shortly after his death, by contrast, admitted the novelist to a place in their scheme of things but only as an *enfant terrible*, who, according to Valbuena Prat, was "un escritor de fama pasajera y de superficiales pretensiones ambiciosas . . . despidió una estela de luminosidad universal, pero transitoria".** The right-wing Torrente Ballester was more harsh: "Era un típico burgués de izquierdas" who "careció . . . de cualquier virtud espiritual o intelectual. Su ideario (si tuvo alguno) es deleznable".†† Perhaps more obfuscating is the well-intentioned whitewashing of C.

---

‡*Cuadernos Hispanoamericanos*, 216 (1967), 507–520.

*D. L. Shaw, 'The Anti-Romantic Reaction in Spain', *MLR*, 63 (1968), 606–11.

†G. G. Brown, Review of W. T. Pattison's *El naturalismo español* (Madrid, 1965), *MLR*, 64 (1969), 200.

‡‡'El caso Blasco Ibáñez', *Hispania* (U.S.A.), 52 (1969), 97–102.

**Historia de la literatura española*, III, Barcelona, 1937, p.436.

† *Literatura española contemporánea*, Madrid, 1949, p.179. See also N. González Ruiz, *La literatura española*, Madrid, 1943, p.111, and *En esta hora*, Madrid, 1925, pp. 175–76; E. Gómez de Baquero, 'Las novelas de Blasco Ibáñez' *Cultura Española*, 12 (1908), 939.

Pitollet (*4*) and J. M. Meliá* who attempted to return the black sheep to the fold. Meliá, for example, commented in 1963 that:

> Blasco, en verdad, contra la religión, no era más que un escandaloso. Era como uno de esos niños revoltosos, rústicos y traviesos que se desahogan apedreando los cristales de la vecindad, provocando a los niños de su edad para excitarlos a la pelea,

a comment that hardly coincides with the facts.

The point at issue here is that the emphasis laid by critics on the liberal and anti-capitalist thesis or the anti-religious determinist view said to be contained in *La barraca* and other novels has obscured the fact that in them Blasco Ibáñez may have been arguing along other lines. It is possible that he was exploring the position of the working-class man of energy and idealism in a society controlled by forces, natural and social, beyond his control, and that he is as much if not more interested in such a man and his problem as he is in condemning the society or protesting at a universe controlled by iron laws. In general terms one might chart in the Valencian novels, beginning with *Arroz y tartana* (1894) and ending with *Cañas y barro* (1902), the rise and ultimate rejection of this theme. In the early novels (*Arroz y tartana, Flor de mayo* [1895]), he is concerned with the position of man in an urban or quasi-urban society with a strong bias towards sociopolitical concerns. In *Entre naranjos* (1900), and especially *Cañas y barro*, he emphasises the way in which man acts at the bidding of an all-powerful nature that works its will through the medium of local conditions. "Man is crushed by nature", observed S. H. Eoff of the later novel, "not in his separateness from it but because he is one with it" (*14*, 119). *La barraca* is perhaps the most interesting work of this period because it stands between these two emphases. This equipoise of interest probably accounts for the instinctive appeal the novel has for the majority of critics who agree unanimously that, in the words of E. Gómez de Baquero in 1908, "*La barraca* pasa con justicia por una de las mejores novelas de Blasco Ibáñez". While the majority stress the success of narrative or stylistic features, few have paused to ponder what *La*

*Blasco Ibáñez, novelista, Valencia, 1963, p.60.

barraca offers in terms of ideas. What will explain the continued popularity of a novel that had sold over 112,000 copies by January 1928 (when the author died) and now has exceeded one million? The success of *La barraca* outside Spain may be due to the fact that the novel transcends specific reference to embrace universal concerns. While, in the words of Vázquez Cey, it recounts "claramente al porvenir cuanta fue la amargura social de sus días", it also tells of "las limitaciones – perennes – de la solidaridad entre los hombres".* It is, as Azorín noted in his essay 'Valencia', "una novela sin tesis parcializante".

If Blasco Ibáñez has achieved considerable recognition outside Spain, in his own country, since roughly the end of the Civil War, he has been the victim of what amounts to a conspiracy of silence. By contrast with the pre-Civil War situation outlined above, for over twenty years Blasco Ibáñez has been neglected by Spanish establishment critics. It was not until 1967, the year of the centenary of the novelist's birth, that the silence was momentarily broken. This event became the rallying point of those few Spanish-speaking critics, Valencian and expatriate, who were anxious to restore Blasco Ibáñez to his proper place in the literary histories of Spain. This year saw the reprinting of E. Gascó Contell's biography of 1921 (*1*), the publication of J. León Roca's major study on the life and works, *Vicente Blasco Ibáñez* (*7*) and a spate of articles. Why should such a campaign be called for? "Porque, no nos engañemos," wrote Juan Ignacio Ferreras in 1967†, "en la España de hoy y en la Valencia de hoy, Blasco Ibáñez es un tabú. Blasco Ibáñez no posee una calle con su nombre en su ciudad natal, ni una placa ni una estatua; la mayor parte de sus obras han sido desterradas de la biblioteca de la Universidad de Valencia . . ." In the same year, in the leading literary journal *Insula* (No. 354), José Domingo noted sadly :

Muy pocos libros conmemorativos, unos biográficos, unos críticos, con preferencia de escritores o investigadores coterráneos. Algunos artículos más o menos superficiales . . . silencio casi absoluto en las publicaciones de carácter nacional, así como

*'*La barraca*, novela mediterránea', *Humanidades* (Argentina), 24 (1934), 311.
†*Les Langues Néo-Latines*, 180 (1967), 21.

en los círculos intelectuales del país. El novelista valenciano ha sido casi olímpicamente ignorado y nadie ha mostrado el menor interés por contribuir a sacarlo de ese purgatorio al que lo han condenado.

In spite of the considerable achievements of León Roca, the early novels of Blasco Ibáñez still await objective critical assessment.‡ Given the failure of the centenary celebrations, Betoret Paris' plea cannot remain unheeded:

ante la evidente injusticia con que ha sido tratado, ¿podremos negarle una revisión objetiva de su obra, una reevaluación de su novelística sin actitudes preconcebidas, que en conciencia merece?*

"To my mind", wrote E. A. Peers, shortly after Blasco Ibáñez's death, "there can be no doubt whatever that, when Blasco Ibáñez's ephemeral, ostentatious novels are wholly forgotten, . . . the really great novels of his youth . . . will re-emerge from the shadows and regain their rightful place in literature." It is hoped that this study will in some measure further that end.

‡M. Xandro's recent *V. Blasco Ibáñez*, Madrid, 1971, offers only the most scanty and general of introductions to Blasco Ibáñez and his work. It relies heavily on the pioneer work of Gascó Contell (*1*).

*'El caso Blasco Ibáñez', *Hispania* (U.S.A.), 52 (1969), 102.

All of Blasco Ibáñez's biographers are in agreement, not only that *La barraca* is probably his best work, but also that it established his literary fame. The details of this meteoric rise from obscurity to European, and subsequently world-wide, renown are well-known. Less known is the history of the novel's genesis.

In the prologue to the 1925 edition of the novel, Blasco Ibáñez recalled that *La barraca* was written between October and December of 1898. J. L. León Roca's study (*12*) has shown that the author's memory was at fault, and argues for March-November 1898. Sifting the files of *El Pueblo*, León Roca found the following note in the number for 2 October 1898 : "De mediados a fines del presente mes comenzará a publicar 'El Pueblo' en su folletín la nueva novela de Blasco Ibáñez, 'La barraca'." In fact the novel began to appear a month later on 6 November in ten episodes. The serial concluded on 16 November when the complete novel was published in Valencia by the author's friend Francisco Sempere. Further information concerning the subsequent fortunes of the novel is to be found in an interview given to Enrique González Fiol (writing under the *nom-de-plume* of 'El bachiller Corchuelo') in *Por esos mundos* (No. 194) in March 1911 :

> Tirada a 700 ejemplares al precio de 1 peseta, *La barraca* se vendió poco — y creo que ni siquiera se hubiera agotado la edición, si no me la tradujera Hérelle al francés, lo cual tuvo por consecuencia su publicación en *El Liberal* de Madrid y la popularidad, que no ha cesado de crecer, de dicha novela.

Again the author's comment needs re-touching. A number of critics perpetuate the story that Georges Hérelle, teacher and translator, bought the volume on the station at San Sebastián while returning home to Bayonne, and that Hérelle's translation made Blasco Ibáñez's name in France and Spain. In fact the letter asking permission to translate, received on 22 March 1899, was at first ignored. When the author gave permission, *Terres maudites* was serialised in *La Revue de Paris* in October-November 1901 and was quickly followed by the Calmann-Lévy (Paris) and Prometeo (Valencia) editions, "de que data el comienzo del renombre mundial de Vicente Blasco Ibáñez" (*4*, 15). Yet by May 1899 critical acclaim had warranted a serialisation in *El Liberal* and a second edition of the novel was published in Madrid. It may be that Blasco Ibáñez's francophilia led him to create the myth that it fell to the energetic and Republican French rather than reactionary Spain to recognise his talent. Certainly, French critics and the scholars of the *Bulletin Hispanique* acclaimed this fiery Republican. He had, after all, drawn international attention to his own political affiliations when, through the columns of *El Pueblo* on 15 February 1898, he organised a letter of solidarity with Zola after the hostility over Zola's *J'Accuse* (13 January 1898) (*12*, 9-10 & *8*, 14). Perhaps he preferred their support to the timidity of Spanish liberals. Blasco Ibáñez's début has never been fully investigated and the reason why French scholars should be more attracted at the time to the Valencian rather than to the giants of the generation – Unamuno, Ganivet, Baroja – has never been elucidated.

León Roca has investigated the sources and genesis of the novel. The 'accepted versions' of the circumstances surrounding the composition of *La barraca* are contained in the interviews with González Fiol (1911) and the second volume of J. M. Carretero's *Lo que sé por mí. Confesiones del siglo* (Madrid, n.d.). Further details are given by the author in the 1925 edition. In short, as a result of his participation in an anti-Cuban War demonstration in 1895, a warrant for his arrest was issued. He was forced into hiding for four days before his escape to Italy. "Obligado a no moverme de aquel sitio incómodo", he recorded, "durante cuatro días consecutivos, distraí mi ocio forzado con la composición de un cuento que titulé *Venganza árabe,* cuyas cuartillas dejé al salir de mi escondrijo, en un estante de dicha taberna" (Fiol). Blasco Ibáñez went on to recall that during the electoral campaign for Cullera when he was elected deputy in March 1898, the story was returned to him. He first thought of sending it unchanged to *El Liberal* (by 1925 this had become *El Heraldo de Madrid*), but

decided to rework and amplify the tale, since it seemed to him
rather dry and concise. León Roca accepts the story, but corrects
the date 1895 to March 1896. The discrepancies between accounts
centre mainly on the title of the story : *Venganza árabe* in Fiol,
morisca in Carretero, *moruna* in the 1925 edition. What is more
important is that the genesis of *La barraca* is the best documented
of all the novels. To the simple question by González Fiol in 1911
"¿Qué le inspiró *La barraca*?", the author replied : "La realidad.
Allí hay más realidad que imaginación : *La barraca* es de todas
mis obras la que tiene más historia." To Carretero he remarked :
"Mi novela *La barraca* tiene su historia."

What is the 'historia'? González Fiol recorded that :

> A una hermana de Blasco que tenía doce años menos que él
> (ocho según León Roca), la criaba una nodriza huertana. Su
> madre y él, cuando iban a visitarla, a la huerta, veían allá, un
> poco distante del camino, unos campos llenos de maleza
> incultos en medio de otros de esmeralda, siempre lozanos y
> bien trabajados ... En medio de aquellos campos de desolación,
> había una barraca caída. Su visión le causaba una impresión
> tristísima, hasta sentía miedo al pasar por allí.

This is almost what Pepeta sees and feels as she returns from
Valencia in chapter I of the novel. Carretero's interview amplifies
the above, when Blasco Ibáñez relates :

> Es en suma, una historia vivida, pues había visto yo muchas
> veces, cuando niño, cerca de Valencia y no lejos del Cementerio,
> aquellos campos utilizados más tarde para el ensanche urbano,
> y la lucha entre el propietario y los labriegos, originada por un
> trágico suceso y amplificada después en conflictos y violencias,
> me era familiar.

This account is substantially repeated in 1925.

León Roca properly asks what 'trágico suceso' took place in
1875, the year the author would have visited the *nodriza huertana*.

> En 1879 la huerta valenciana, pese a los panegiristas más
> encendidos, sufría una de las más violentas revoluciones. La
> originó, sin duda, un implacable régimen de sequía que estaba
> durando cuatro años (7, 212-13, & *12*, 16).

Combing the newspaper files in Valencia for the years 1875-79, León Roca has uncovered vital information that gives life to the anecdotes about *La barraca's* genesis. In brief, the prolonged drought brought extreme hardship to workers and landlords alike. *Las Provincias* recorded on 28 March 1879 that : "Los propietarios del llano . . . están alarmadísimos, pues esperan ver perdidas las cosechas si no las favorecen las lluvias." Three days later *El Mercantil Valenciano* agreed that without early rains the future seemed bleak. By June of that year the Tribunal de las aguas could hardly maintain its authority and an appeal was made to the Civil Governor for police help. Late in the same month *Las Provincias* again reflected the worsening situation :

> Cuatro años hace que se pierden las cosechas por falta de lluvias . . . Hay que pintar con exactos colores la desesperada situación de los pobres labradores, que se están alimentando de yerbas silvestres, y pidiendo a Dios que no les falten; . . . hay que decir que hasta los propietarios, en otro tiempo algo acomodados, están reducidos a la miseria.

From natural disaster came social disaster. The peasants, with no resources to sustain them in crisis and ruined by drought, refused collectively to pay the San Juan rental to landlords who had funds to fall back on. Such was the militancy that even the traditional gifts were withheld. The owner-tenant relationship rapidly became one of equals, the man who worked the land claiming equal rights with its owner. Those 'blacklegs' who broke the collective resolve became the subjects of persecution, their *barracas* burned, their crops damaged, their beasts attacked. When the forces of law and order arrived no witnesses to the outrages could be found, either out of fear of reprisal or out of solidarity. Labour called from outside soon left for fear of attack. This, then, is the substance of the events of 1879 which provided the raw material for the novel. León Roca correctly observed that :

> Este episodio de la huelga de los colonos, que los historiadores han tratado de olvidar, debió conocerlo Blasco Ibáñez en sus menores detalles desde la infancia. Tal vez, sin él proponérselo, a los treinta y un años, brotaron de nuevo los retazos a aquella historia olvidada, reavivada en la barraca de Almácera,

cuando huía de la policía, y fundidos en él tomaron forma artística en la novela que lo inmortalizó (*12*, 20).

There is also every likelihood that the sympathiser with whom Blasco Ibáñez was sheltering had been a witness to the disasters of 1875-79.

Blasco Ibáñez was also explicit about the methods of documentation and digestion of his material. C. Pitollet has recorded that the novelist was wont to destroy preparatory notes and early drafts. We have, therefore, little or no information concerning the creative *modus operandi*. A letter written to Julio Cejador in March 1918* sheds some light on the problem. Speaking of artistic creation in terms of childbirth, much as García Lorca and other writers have done, Blasco Ibáñez describes the genesis and gradual coalescence of ideas and impressions that go to make a work of art:

> Se forman en mí por el procedimiento de la bola de nieve. Una sensación, una idea, no buscadas, surgidas de los limbos de lo subconsciente, sirven de núcleo, y en torno de ellas se amontonan nuevas observaciones y sensaciones almacenadas en ese mismo subconsciente, sin que uno se haya dado cuenta de ello. El que verdaderamente es novelista posee una imaginación semejante a una máquina fotográfica, con el objetivo eternamente abierto. Con la misma inconsciencia de la máquina, sin enterarse de ello, recoge en la vida diario fisonomías, gestos, ideas, sensaciones, guardándolas sin saber que las posee.

One might say that those impressions gathered in 1875 seemed to have lain dormant, to have been revived in 1896 and again in 1898. What is perhaps most interesting here is the problem the author chooses to discuss. In both 1896 and 1898 we find a common denominator: radical political action. Blasco Ibáñez was organising the offensive against the Cuban war, embroiled in Republican campaigning and actively engaged in Valencian civic affairs. On his return from exile in Italy in July 1896, he dedicated himself almost entirely throughout the rest of the year to the anti-War effort. In August alone he wrote ten leading

*The letter is reproduced in Cejador's *Historia de la lengua y litreatura castellanas*, IX, Madrid, 1920, pp. 471-78.

articles on the subject in *El Pueblo*. He was arrested on 14 September, not on account of the warrant issued for the demonstration on 8 March, but because of his "intemperantes escritos". The charge of the Consejo de Guerra ran as follows:

> Consta en autos y además está en la conciencia de toda persona sensata de esta capital, que don Vicente Blasco Ibáñez ejerce tal influencia en el ánimo de la clase proletaria, que pudiera muy bien asegurarse que la tiene sugestionada con sus intemperantes escritos que diariamente publica el periódico titulado *El Pueblo* (*12*, 7).

On 26 September 1896, he was sentenced to two years' imprisonment. By 1898 he was an *habitué* of Valencian gaols, regarded as an enemy of the system and, according to Just Gimeno in 1931, 'molt renom'. So dangerous and powerful a figure was Blasco Ibáñez as editor of *El Pueblo* that despite his immunity as *diputado* he was illegally arrested by the military Governor on 27 October 1898 as he was about to lead the masses into open confrontation with the city fathers over the *affaire Touchet* and the Cuban War (*12*, 12-13).

The novel was first drafted in an atmosphere of high conspiracy while the author still suffered from wounds received in a duel fought in the previous January. It was re-drafted and completed amid the uproar of the offices of *El Pueblo* and political activism. One can but marvel that the novel is so well made. C. Pitollet has reminded us that:

> Todas estas obras, que de común acuerdo se ha dado en definir como las más lozanas y las más atrayentes de nuestro autor, fueron compuestas, sin embargo, entre la baraunda de una sala de redacción de diario popular y sin otra pretensión que la de distraer a la plebe que formaba su clientela fiel. He aquí lo que ningún crítico había pensado decir, y merecía hacerse la atención (*4*, 50).

What is strange is that this turmoil barely ruffles the surface of the novel. There is, for example, only one oblique reference to the Cuban War, but even this remains undeveloped. In chapter IX the family, at the height of material prosperity, can relax for a moment and anticipate the fulfillment of their labours and aspirations. What Teresa looks for in prosperity is significant in the context of the above:

> Todo exige un principio, y si los tiempos eran buenos, a este dinero se uniría otro y otro, y ¡quién sabe si al llegar los chicos a la edad de las quintas podría librarlos con sus ahorros de ir a servir el rey como soldados! (145).

There is no indication that the mother feels that this system is evil or socially unjust. She accepts it without question. How unlike the author's leader column, 'Carne de pobres', in *El Pueblo* of 19 August 1898 addressed to the mothers of Valencia and penned alongside the novel:

> . . . y cuando el hijo es ya un hombre que contribuye con su jornal al mantenimiento de la que tanto se sacrificó por él, cuando en el mismo hogar comienza a acariciarse la esperanza de una mayor comodidad, se presenta el Estado con sus absurdos privilegios de clase, para decirle a la madre:
> " – ¿Tienes mil quinientas pesetas? ¿No? Pues dame tu hijo. Sois pobres y esto basta. Lleváis sobre vuestra frente ese sello de maldición social que os hace eternos esclavos del dolor. En la paz, debéis sufrir resignados y agotar vuestro cuerpo poco a poco para que una minoría viva tranquila y placenteramente sin hacer nada; en la guerra: debéis morir para que los demás, que por el dinero están libres de tal peligro, puedan ser belicosos desde su casa. Resignaos: siempre ha habido un rebaño explotado para bien y tranquilidad de los de arriba."

This is the fiery radical writing as a deputy without fear of censure. Only an order from the Cortes itself could effectively silence him. Yet León Roca's judgement, referring to this new-found immunity, cannot be accepted unchallenged.

> Este estado de ánimo, aparte de la satisfacción de verse elevado a la dignidad de representante popular, al cabo de tantos años de lucha, es el que cabe adivinar en Blasco Ibáñez cuando se decide a escribir *La barraca* (*12*, 13).

There is little evidence to suggest that the novel was a literary interpretation of the questions aired in the pages of *El Pueblo*, a propaganda piece against the inequalities of conscription or an anti-war document. It may be that the novel served as a palliative to the catechising editorials of *El Pueblo* so that he could produce a more balanced view of the human predicament. As we shall see, C. Pitollet's judgement that:

> Cuando vivió en Valencia, compuso sus novelas valencianas, . . . manifestando en su autor un alma violenta y sencilla, semejante a la de sus protagonistas y una mentalidad un poco provinciana (4, 187),

is as wide of the mark as those of Blasco Ibáñez's detractors.

3 La barraca *as a realist novel*

Of the many definitions of Realism in the mid-nineteenth century, that of Edmond Duranty in *Réalisme* (1856-57) seems to have been among the most widely accepted:

> Realism commits itself to an exact, complete, and sincere reproduction of the social milieu, of the contemporary world . . . this reproduction should therefore be as simple as possible so that anyone may understand it.

This high-minded definition, while enthusiastically glossed by Zola in *Le Roman expérimental* (1880), was soon to be the centre of a fierce polemic. Leaving aside the confusion between Realism and Naturalism, a problem tackled in G. J. Becker's masterly introduction to *Documents of Modern Literary Realism* (Princeton, 1963)*, let us examine why the question of the 'reproduction of a social milieu' should have caused such a flutter in the critical dovecotes. However sincere an artist's reproduction of reality, that reality must always be filtered through the writer's own particular convictions and prejudices. What happened when Duranty's idealism resulted in a failure to understand the society or, more pertinently, caused a fundamental disagreement with accepted reproductions of reality? One might say that traditionalist writers presented their reality within a framework that reflected their own conservative and reactionary sentiments. One cannot underestimate the impact made by liberal writers when they presented their realistic vision of the world in terms that not only dissented from the traditional world view, but reproduced society in terms radically opposed to that view. Such is the case with Blasco Ibáñez.

As W. T. Pattison has ably demonstrated, the new Realist and

*See also L. R. Furst and P. N. Skrine, *Naturalism*, London, Methuen, 1971, and D. Grant, *Realism*, London, Methuen, 1970.

Naturalist ideas were enthusiastically absorbed in the late 1870s.†
However, that initial euphoria was quickly exhausted. Under the
inherent contradiction outlined above and sharpened by divisions
that were ideological rather than artistic, the conviction soon
emerged that the new ideas were in some way demoralizing.
This will explain much of the scandalised alarm surrounding
Blasco Ibáñez's novels. However much literary theorists like
González Serrano and Giner de los Ríos believed that the novel
would provide a means of analysing and ultimately regenerating
contemporary society, the liberal 'reproduction of the social
milieu' seemed too dangerous. In the ethos of Restoration socio-
politics, writers swiftly reacted against radical idealism and what
they saw as incipient socialism, putting forward the view that the
business of art was not to depict contemporary reality. The
bourgeois anti-revolutionary enthusiasm of the leading novelists,
following the lead of Cánovas' politics, was directed along new
channels. The search for truth was subordinated to respect for
received ideas. Art, all too often relying on the power of regionalist description, was looked on as a sort of imaginative consola-
tion for the inroads of sceptical liberalism. The emphasis on
imagination and on "literary technique or mode, it was believed,
would deflect writers from acquiring dangerous ideological
preoccupations".* Blasco Ibáñez's refusal to write in this spirit,
like the refusal by Galdós, caused an immediate drawing of the
battlelines described in chapter I. As E. Sebastià has noted with
considerable acumen, "the Spanish bourgeoisie . . . was too
fragile and too new to remain insensible to the irritations
produced by a writer who refused to adjust to the artistic models
of the novel consumed by the dominant social class" (*13*, 26-27).

Blasco Ibáñez's apologists have in general lauded his gifts as a
regionalist writer and his power of description. Yet, in the final
analysis, Blasco Ibáñez's *costumbrismo* is something of a critical

---

†*El naturalismo español*, Madrid, Gredos, 1965. See also G. Davis, 'The Critical
Reception of Naturalism in Spain before *La cuestión palpitante*', HR, XXII (1954),
97–108, and 'The Spanish Debate over Idealism and Realism before the Impact
of Zola's Naturalism', *PMLA*, 84 (1969), 1649–56.

*G. G. Brown, Review of Pattison, *El naturalismo español*, MLR, 64 (1969),
200–02.

red-herring. *Costumbrismo* may be loosely defined as an artistic reproduction of the manners, customs, attitudes and locale of a given regional *patria chica*.* The realism of the 1870s came to prominence under this guise when the novel developed beyond the *cuadro de costumbres*. Within a short time the artistic presentation of *costumbres* was subordinated to a specific ideological end : it refracted and filtered the so-called 'realistic presentation' through the prism of Catholic and political orthodoxy. The *cuadro de costumbres* provided an ideal vehicle for conservative ideas. Such 'realism' becomes the nostalgic evocation of a Spain where traditional values are hallowed and accepted and each person knows his place in society.

It is clear that Blasco Ibáñez would be unlikely to side with this type of reactionary sentiment and, indeed, he has generally been categorised as hostile to it. Yet for all the militancy of his writings his work seems to have partaken of the general currents that were dominant in the 1880s and 90s. While there certainly remains much of *Krausista*† optimism in his crude analysis of social ills and, one supposes, the hope for a regenerated society, there are moments when the social and the naturalist theses seem to give way to a starry-eyed idealism. E. Sebastià has

---

*For a general account of *costumbrismo*, see J. F. Montesinos, *Introducción a una historia de la novela en España en el siglo XIX*, Valencia, 1955 and his *Costumbrismo y novela*, Madrid, 1960.

†*Krausismo*, introduced from Germany into Spain by J. Sanz del Río in the 1840s, had by the 1860s brought about a small-scale 'Reformation'. The new philosophy comprised a combination of the different forms of rationalist thought in politics, religion and education, and stood in opposition to traditional scholasticism. For all its theorisation, *Krausismo* was less a question of ideas than an attitude to life. From it the leaders of the First Republic (and especially Giner de los Ríos, the founder of the Institución Libre de Enseñanza) forged a lay spirituality with rigid moral principles and a deep faith in the possibility of spiritual and material progress through education. Sanz del Río and Giner enjoined their disciples to do good for the sake of good as a divine precept. Thus a strong religious sense pervades *Krausista* thought since every useful work was ultimately a revelation of God's goodness and the realisation of the designs of providence. Their philosophy incurred the enmity of Catholic conservatism. They were accused, among other things, of disseminating heretical ideas and corrupting the youth of Spain. See J. López Morillas, *El krausismo español*, Mexico, 1956; J. B. Trend, *The Origins of Modern Spain*, Cambridge, 1934; M. Menéndez y Pelayo, *Historia de los heterodoxos españoles*, vol. III, Madrid, 1881; V. Cacho Viu, *La Institución libre de enseñanza*, vol. I, Madrid, 1962.

condemned his fellow Valencian for occasionally painting a false picture of the *huerta* (*13*, 67). Now and then in the novel the descriptions of the *huerta* and the peasants have a distinct echo of the *costumbrismo* of a Trueba, a Fernán Caballero or a Pereda. C. Blanco Aguinaga has already drawn attention to the "evidente costumbrismo" (*10*, 192) of *La barraca*, and E. Betoret Paris has deemed it sufficiently dominant to warrant a monograph (*9*). In chapter IX when there is a lull in the animosity of the *huertanos* after the tragic death of Pascualet the atmosphere is depicted in Edenic terms. There, by dint of virtuous labour, Christian suffering and acceptance of God's will, all is bounty, stability and peaceful order. Man is in harmony with the universe.

> Atravesando la vega en las horas de más sol, cuando ardía la atmósfera a moscas y abejorros zumbaban pesadamente, sentía una impresión de bienestar ante esta barraca limpia y fresca . . . Había que dar gracias a Dios, que le permitía al fin vivir tranquilo en aquel paraíso (145).

The same might be argued of the description of the restored *barraca* in chapter III (62), the description of the girls returning home whose "desfile daba a la huerta Valenciana algo de sabor bíblico" (94), and the term "Arcadia moruna" (54).

Yet there is nothing in the description that shows the specific influence of *costumbrista* technique. It seems more the product of the same mentality that produced the *costumbrismo* which these passages seem to echo. That is, it is an ideological more than a technical borrowing. This puts the reader on the alert. It may be that he was using conservative *costumbrismo* against his orthodox contemporaries. Pereda celebrates the peasantry of the Montaña in terms of their unthinking and uncritical acceptance of traditional values uncontaminated by liberal thought from the city. In essence, the nineteenth-century version of *alabanza de aldea*. Paradoxically, Blasco Ibáñez also praises the peasant, but from his own distinctly radical viewpoint. His descriptions could be a corrective to their view. He may have been debunking *costumbrismo* as Galdós had done in *Doña Perfecta*. Again and again Arcadian tranquillity collapses into violence. Batiste is lulled into a false sense of security and sees life in Arcadian terms.

His vision is a false one as the subsequent incident at casa de Copa shows all too clearly. Batiste has been conditioned by the ruling classes, by his education and social experience, to pursue such a dream. Blasco Ibáñez may be warning his readers of the dangers of a reproduction of the social milieu in such rosy terms. Material prosperity could be a carrot offered to hold the working classes from dissent. The calm of the Fuente and the outrage on Roseta, like the ritual of the horse-buying and the death of Pascualet, are other cases in point. In the former the "sabor bíblico" gives way to "dolor y rabia" (94-97); in the second the thrill of the haggling, the intoxicating atmosphere of the gypsy fair, give way to the death agonies of Pascualet. Perhaps the peasant could create a true Arcadia if he were left alone and unexploited. There is an essential difference of approach here in contrast to the *costumbristas*. The author's major concern is with the historical and socio-economic situation, however much he appears to present simple *cuadros*.

Yet, despite the above, and the general acclaim of Blasco Ibáñez's 'stark realism', it would be unwise to argue that the Valencian stood against the new artistic currents of the 1890s. He was certainly no 'scientific' observer or theorist in the way advocated by Renan in *L'Avenir de la science* (1848-9) (translated into Spanish by *El Pueblo* in 1903), or the realist that Zola and even Galdós became. His biographer C. Pitollet recorded that:

> El que no ha tomado nunca ninguna nota para la preparación de sus novelas, no sabe decir nada que valga la pena en cuanto se trata de montar ese aparato crítico que es como la armazón de toda obra no ya de imaginación, sino de ciencia (*4*, 13-14).

Indeed, the novelist's own comments to Pitollet and to the critic Julio Cejador both indicate that he was appealing more to the imaginative faculty. As far as documentation is concerned it would appear, if we are to believe the novelist himself, that he assimilated rather than empirically documented his novels:

> Me sumo . . . en la vida y me codeo con el público de la calle, con las muchedumbres, buenas y malas. En una palabra, trato de asimilarme las mil variedades diversas de lo real. . . . Es eso lo que torna a crear la actividad productora (*4*, 67-8).

In the famous letter to Cejador he went so far as to devolve some responsibility onto the reader. Such a statement undermines the view of art based on empirical observation; it is a renegation of the spirit of Zolaism.

> El pintor seguro de su mano y de su imaginación no coloca explicaciones al margen de su obra. El público verá claramente lo que quiso expresar en el lienzo, como quiso expresarlo. Y si el público da una docena de versiones diferentes, ¿quién sabe si la definitiva, la que acaba por triunfar, no es superior a la que pensó el artista?

It is regrettable that Blasco Ibáñez has so little to say on the problems of documentary realism. It may be that the artificial dichotomy between imagination and reality that emerged in the 1880s forced a number of writers into ambivalent or paradoxical attitudes. Yet reinforced by the hypnotic prestige of scientific exactitude there emerged a number of bizarre technical problems, one being the place of the narrator in an experimental novel.

Speaking of Zola's *L'Argent*, Alas had pleaded convincingly in the *Ensayos y revistas* of 1892 for the ability of impersonal narration to express adequately the sadness of life. But as S. Beser and B. W. Ife have shown, Alas was aware of the inherent fallacy of documentary realism, especially when the author knows that the suggestive power of fiction lies in another direction.* In a 'scientific' novel there can be no place for an author's views and tastes, no emotional reactions, no ethical standards. Even Zola, grudgingly, was forced to beg the question of documentary realism in his dictum that "une oeuvre est un coin de la création vu à travers un tempérament". Thus literature, as Alas and others realised, was concerned not only with the relationship between the author and reality, properly the realm of observation, but more pertinently with the relationship between the author and the work. "It is the artistic ordering and presentation of observed facts to reveal their implicit significance. A novel, then, can perform two tasks at once; it can accurately document the author's

*S. Beser, *Leopoldo Alas, crítico literario*, Madrid, 1968 and B. W. Ife, 'Idealism and Materialism in Clarín's *La Regenta*', *Revue de Littérature Comparée*, 44 (1970), 273–295.

society and reveal by the very technique of documentation the author's personal response to being part of that society."† There is a relationship between experience and expression. It is for us, the literary critics, to be sensitive to the expression so that we may better understand the author's viewpoint. It may be that it is to this aspect of literary creation that Blasco Ibáñez is referring in the letter to Cejador when he shifts some of the onus of interpretation on to his reading public. Given the paucity of serious pronouncements on literature and literary criticism by Blasco Ibáñez we can only speculate.‡ This question, however, merits serious consideration, especially when we find Blasco Ibáñez now employing one literary mode, now another.

We do know, thanks to E. Betoret Paris' *El costumbrismo en la obra de Blasco Ibáñez* (9), that the major descriptive passages have a basis in observed reality. According to Betoret Paris all the various scenes are faithful descriptions of the original settings. On his visit to the *huerta* to document his book he reported that "estuvimos en la taberna de *Copa*, que con ligeras modificaciones está lo mismo que cuando la describe Blasco" (318). In the same way he authenticated the account of the Tribunal* (220-25) and the Fuente de la Reina (320). The horse-fair is, as Betoret Paris admits, a mixture of what he chooses to call a *cuadro de costumbres*, the telling detail and documentary realism:

> Esta escena del mercado de animales no es esencial para el argumento. . . . Pero es de suma importancia en una novela de costumbres valencianas. Por ella conocemos mejor a uno de los principales protagonistas, sus reacciones, su habilidad, el lugar destacado que ocupe el caballo en la vida . . . (9, 153).

The *cuadros*, then, are more than the result of a love for a particular *patria chica*; they are carefully woven into the story itself.

---

†Ife, 274.

‡The *Discursos literarios* (Valencia, 1966) reproduce a number of public lectures delivered on literary topics from 1909 onwards. Given the public they were aimed at, and the fact that they afforded a platform and an income, their quality as documents of exegesis barely transcends the anecdotic and the superficial.

*For a precise account of the Tribunal, see R. Gayano Lluch, *Els furs de València*, Valencia, 1930, p.222 and V. Giner Boira, *El tribunal de las aguas de la vega de Valencia*, Valencia, 1953.

Unlike Pereda's self-satisfied celebration of the traditionalism of
the Montaña and its customs, where the scenes are rarely inte-
grated with the narrative, Blasco Ibáñez's scenes, although he has
a different viewpoint, one of working-class idealism, are fully
absorbed into the body of the novel. "Está Blasco", argues Blanco
Aguinaga, "en sus primeras novelas a enorme distancia de Pereda,
de Valera o de la Pardo Bazán, puesto que ninguno de aquellos
costumbristas había tratado a fin de siglo su realidad local desde
una perspectiva histórica y social remotamente parecida a la del
valenciano" (*10*, 192). This is crucial.

The customs described, especially the *albaet** with its implicit
superstition, are also authentic. They form an ethnological
account "para que se conozca mejor la región en épocas sucesivas"
(*9*, 203). The same is argued of the "patriarcales costumbres"
and Batiste's reaction to Roseta's flirtation with Tonet, "la terrible majestad del padre latino, señor absoluto de sus hijos" (77).
Of the love relationship Betoret Paris remarks that "la mujer
valenciana . . . no es la activa en amores" (*9*, 186). True to this,
the *huertanas* and Roseta are depicted as models of simple peasant
virtue. Rosario is only led to betray that virtue through the avarice
of capitalism. Tonet and Roseta's affair is "inocente" (93); the
silk-girls, though flirtatious, allow no physical contact with the
young *huertanos* (83).

Authentic, too, according to Betoret Paris, is the Catalan
dialect of the novel :

> Parte de su técnica es el uso del valenciano en sus escritos, pues
> es evidente que con objeto de dar mayor realismo a sus crea-
> ciones puso en boca de muchos personajes las expresiones en su
> lengua materna que tan eficazmente ayudan a crear un am-
> biente adecuado . . . El uso de esta lengua regional es otro
> medio para localizar la acción y aumentar la verosimilitud del
> relato (*9*, 278).

Antonio Espina, agreeing, has remarked that "el diálogo es uno

---

*See Cheyne, pp. 192–3: "diminutive of Valencian *albat* (=*párvulo*). The
term is applied to a child who dies before reaching the age of reason, by which
the Roman Catholic Church means the age at which a human being begins to be
morally responsible for his actions, normally at about seven years." The term
also embraces the special preparation of the corpse for burial.

de los grandes dominios del novelista que sabe recoger con fide-
lidad".*

The characters, too, apparently had counterparts in real life.
"*Copa* el tabernero", asserts Betoret Paris, "es un tabernero con
hechos de valiente que Blasco conoció siendo pequeño" (9, 39).
In a letter, Blasco Ibáñez's son told Betoret Paris in 1955 that

> Pimentó vivía, en efecto, en la huerta de Alboraya. Tiene
> muchos puntos de contacto con un arrendatorio que tenía la
> suegra de Blasco. Como era viuda y vivía sola con su hija, la
> futura esposa del novelista, que entonces era una niña, él se
> aprovechaba de su miedo sacando la navaja para picar el
> tabaco, y cuando ella le preguntaba si pensaba pagar, el salía
> con : ¿Pera qué son les caenes? . . . ¡Pera els homens!† (9, 39).

We are immediately reminded of Pimentó's braggart speech in
casa de Copa and his account of the visits to his *propietaria* Doña
Manuela. He would philosophise and utter the accustomed phil-
ippic against exploitation that earns him the name "el de las
cadenas" (156). Then would follow the implied menace with the
"navaja enorme" (155). Don Mario Blasco also wrote that
"Blasco, siendo muchacho, conoció al tío *Tomba*, el viejo pastor,
antiguo guerrillero de la partida del Flare. Don Joaquín, el
maestro, iba a la Malvarrosa a enseñar a leer al casero de la villa
del autor" (9, 40)‡.

The oblique mention of the War of Independence is accom-
panied by reference to other historical events. The most obvious
is that of the expulsion of the Moors (145) by James I of Aragon
and their final banishment under the edict of Philip III of 1609.
Another is to the *desamortización* of Church property under
Mendizábal in 1837 (37-8).** Important though these references
are, León Roca has shown how much more important is the
implicit history of the novel. The previous chapter has already
touched on the drought and the subsequent quarrels between the
owners and workers in 1875-79. León Roca's detective work has

---

*'Ojeada sobre Blasco Ibáñez', *Revista de Occidente*, 58 (1968), 60.
†¿Para qué son las cadenas? ¡Para los hombres!
‡See also J. Just Gimeno, *Los amigos de Blasco Ibáñez*, Valencia, 1935 and
León Roca, *12*, 15.
**See note on p. 10 above.

uncovered reports of the situation in *Las Provincias,* dated 29 December 1878 and 26 June 1879, which offer an astonishing parallel to the situation developed in the novel. The author always insisted that the novel was inspired by those impressions made on him as an eight-year-old. Yet as one reads *Las Provincias* one cannot but echo León Roca's "diríamos que se había informado en esta carta" (*12*, 18). We have already quoted the report of 26 June 1879 in the previous chapter. In the previous December an anonymous writer wrote:

No es una huelga en que se discuten las condiciones del trabajo agrícolo lo que está sucediendo en Valencia; su verdadero nombre es el de una coalición para eludir el cumplimento de un contrato perfecto.

Niéganse los arrendatarios a pagar la renta del segundo semestre de este año, como ya negaron la correspondiente al primero. . . . Resisten la entrega de los artículos, que, a modo de regalo, hacen desde tiempo inmemorial a los dueños de la tierra, siendo de notar que si antes pudo significar esto el reconocimiento del dominio directo, hoy es además cláusula de contrato, sin ningún carácter de prestación señorial. Colonos hay que acuden a casa del propietario, manifestando tener buena voluntad de pagar las rentas, pero dejan de llevarlas pretextando el temor de verse atacados en sus personas y cosas. Barracas que se incendian, cosechas que se destruyen, plantaciones que se arrancan, . . . atentados contra la seguridad; tales son las manifestaciones de este hecho que produce honda alarma en la población y en la huerta. El incendio, las amenazas, las violencias, son delitos que el Código penal castiga; pero se instruyen procesos, se incoan las causas, y luego viene el sobreseimiento, porque faltan pruebas, y los mismos colones, sea por complicidad o por miedo, nada declaran. Y al lado de todo esto se ve a los dueños temblar ante la idea del desahucio, porque tienen la convicción de que ningún nuevo colono se atreverá a ocupar la tierra desalojada ante el temor, muy fundado, según la experiencia demuestra, de que se lo impida el trabuco de los coaligados.

Pimentó is the incarnation of all these elements of worker opposition, elements which, the reader readily recognises, are faithfully reproduced in the novel. For a more unified effect the collective antagonism is synthesised in a single person. Barret, too, is unable to pay (42), which brings about his eviction and the boycott. After the murder of don Salvador no one will witness against Barret: "nadie habló." "Las barracas hubiesen abierto para él sus últimos escondrijos; las mujeres le habrían ocultado bajo sus faldas" (51). After his sentence the *huerta* becomes a *colación*: "Fue esto un acuerdo tácito de toda la huerta, una conjuración instintiva" (52). The collective 'boicottage popular', as Pitollet terms it, has the same repercussions as the report in *Las Provincias*. Given the harassment of those sent to work the empty lands in the novel, "los dueños de las tierras pidieron protección hasta en los papeles públicos. Y parejas de la Guardia Civil fueron a correr la huerta" (54).

In a letter to the Civil Governor and to the newspapers the Liga de Propietarios complained of the anarchic situation on the *huerta*. "Los colonos en masa, sin distinción", they complained, "se negaron al pago." Crops and *barracas* are being burned, they went on, attacks perpetrated on strike-breakers. *El Mercantil Valenciano* reported the burning of *barracas* on 31 March 1878 near "el Cementerio general". Perhaps it was their ruins that caused such an impression on the young valenciano.* Batiste and Barret are the fictional victims of this historical situation of 1875-79. "Fue su vida una continua batalla con la sequía" relates Blasco Ibáñez of Batiste, "Llovió poco, las cosechas fueron malas *durante cuatro años*" (57). The choice of the qualifying 'cuatro' cannot be purely coincidental. In the same way the growing strength of the landowners at the end of the novel alluded to by the drunken Pimentó – "los amos, conejos miedosos, se habían vuelto ahora lobos intratables" (157) – closely mirrors the decision of the Liga to have the Governor enforce the law and hold the peasants to their contracts. Batiste's successful occupation of the 'blacked' lands has revived the spirits of 'law and order'. Suddenly "se había roto el encanto. Desde que un ladrón 'muerto de hambre' había logrado imponerse a todos ellos, los propietarios se reían" (157). The peasants have lost their position of strength.

---

*See also the autobiographical notes in the prologue to the 1st edition of *Flor de mayo*.

The double burden of natural and social disaster turns peasant passivity into resentment and revolt. Such a close parallel would suggest, as we have remarked before, that although Blasco Ibáñez may have had a vivid memory he also probably refreshed that memory by some basic research. Late in his biography Pitollet contradicts his earlier assertion that Blasco Ibáñez made no preparatory notes. He relates that several novels were carefully documented (*4*, 201). A period in the Valencia archives may well have been another exercise in basic documentation.

Betoret Paris has suggested that the novels were based on personal experience. We know that Blasco Ibáñez was of a poor Aragonese family that had made good in Valencia. Juli Just Gimeno has shown that the author pretended to stem from the rich Cabrerizos*. However, his grandfather had come down to Valencia penniless, like Batiste from Sagunto, and the family had prospered. With this family history he may well have conceived the idea of an *intruso* from the north coming into the *huerta*. This will explain more fully the degree of the "insolencia" of the Borrull activities in chapter III (58-59). The same enmity flares up in casa de Copa (158) and reappears in the antagonism of the neighbourhood at the beginning of chapter X (162).

The social impact of migrant labour from Aragon into Valencia with particular respect to *Arroz y tartana* has been studied by E. Sebastià in *València en les novel·les de Blasco Ibáñez*. He argues that :

> The peculiar psychology of the Aragonese immigrant with work patterns shaped by a hard life whetted by hunger, by a raw climate and a harsh almost barren soil . . . coupled with the favourable economic situation of rapid development and consequent social mobility that the city of adoption offered (*13*, 110)

caused the immigrants to reject their rural proletarian brethren. As they prospered materially, "they became bourgeois identifying with the patrician classes and the hardened Valencian capitalists.

---

*E. Gascó Contell accepts Blasco Ibáñez's story in *Genio y figura de Blasco Ibáñez*, Madrid, 1921, p.18. J. Just Gimeno's *Blasco Ibáñez i València*, Valencia, 1931 shows that the story was untrue.

They were a new and vigorous middle class" (*13*, 110). Their vigour meant that they soon transcended menial labour to adjust to and identify with the ruling classes. On the *huerta*, therefore, they were looked on as a type of bourgeois fifth column, sympathisers with the landowners. Local workers who came were politely warned off; Batiste's presence sparks off an immediate and spontaneous hatred. It may well also explain the awkward shift of sympathy, which we will consider more fully later, from *huertanos* to Batiste. Perhaps Blasco Ibáñez identified more closely with the immigrants, in short, with his own history.

Is the novel allegorical? The peasants do emerge as stereotypes and attitudes rather than living creatures. R. Conte has argued that "Las novelas de Blasco Ibáñez, bien detalladas, interesantes y populares, no son realistas. Son esquemas morales y políticos".* It may be more fruitful to consider how Blasco Ibáñez uses his 'realism', how he orders and presents his observations to reveal their implicit significance. Such ordering, in its turn, reveals the author's response to being a part of the society he is describing.

*R. Conte, 'V. Blasco Ibáñez: Lecciones de un centenario', *Cuadernos Hispanoamericanos*, 216 (1967), 519.

4 La barraca *and naturalism: the power of the earth*

One of the earliest critical clichés applied to Blasco Ibáñez was that of his 'Zolaism' and his 'naturalism'. The first critics of the novel in December 1898 only hinted at such influence. By 1903 one of the lionisers in France had noted that "son admiration pour les naturalistes français a paru compromettre son originalité".* There followed a series of confirmations and refutations of the influence of Le Groupe de Médan† on Blasco Ibáñez, a question that was obscured rather than clarified by the author's coquettish comments. In review after review one finds the arbitrary critical label of 'the Spanish Zola'. Few critics substantiated their claim. One of the earliest, Andrés González Blanco, argued that Zola's influence "es innegable" (6, 582); "si algún novelador naturalista fue en España representante exclusivo del producto francés, es Vicente Blasco Ibáñez" (6, 537). L. Tailhade's refutation, published in 1918, is merely impressionistic. "Rien de plus faux. Blasco Ibáñez est moins dogmatique et plus sincère . . . plus discret, plus nerveux."‡ The debate remained on this superficial level until 1923 when K. Reding's pioneer work 'Blasco Ibáñez and Zola'** appeared. The 1930s saw small skirmishes by J. A. Balseiro and C. Barja (5) whose efforts soon sank under the crushing weight of German erudition.†† A picture gradually emerged of coincidence of style and theme verging on plagiarism, and influences ranging from Flaubert to Rodenbach. Since then

---

*E. Mérimée, 'Blasco Ibáñez et le roman de moeurs provinciales', *Bulletin Hispanique*, 5 (1903), 299.

†A group of five writers—Alexis, Céard, Hennique, Huysmans, Maupassant— who followed the ideas of Zola and met regularly to discuss them with Zola at his country home at Médan, near Paris.

‡'Vicente Blasco Ibáñez', *Hispania* (Paris), 1 (1918), 10–11.

**Hispania* (U.S.A.), 6 (1923), 365–71.

††J. A. Balseiro, 'Vicente Blasco Ibáñez', *Cuatro individualistas de España*, Chapel Hill, 1949; A. Greiner, *Vicente Blasco Ibáñez. Der spanische Zola?*, Jena, 1932; R. Edel, *V. Blasco Ibáñez in seinem Verhältnis zu einigen neuren französischen Romanschriftstellern*, Münster, 1935.

this criticism has been superseded.‡ Speaking specifically of *La barraca* Pitollet rashly insists that the novel "no tolera la menor comparación con Zola" (*4*, 191) and adds that 'Zolaism' has become an overused critical label. The author himself voiced the same view to Cejador. In the letter he is unequivocal but imprecise over the question of influence. "Yo, en mis primeras novelas, sufrí de un modo considerable la influencia de Zola y de la escuela naturalista. En mis primeras novelas nada más." What did he learn from the Naturalists?

Of all the scientific achievements during the nineteenth century one area dominated Zola's interest: the biological sciences. Biology and physiology were important both for the startling nature of the discoveries of Lamarck and Darwin and for their direct relevance to thought and literature. The notions of natural selection and the survival of the fittest ran counter both to idealism and to orthodox religious teaching. Man, in popular terms, suddenly saw himself only a little above the animal kingdom and his life as one of continuous struggle for existence. This view was supported for Zola by the theories of heredity which he discovered in 1868-69 when he read Lucas' *Traité philosophique et physiologique de l'hérédité naturelle* (1850). Heredity, manifesting itself through innate urges and instincts, was also one of the three main principles of the determinism of Hippolyte Taine whose philosophy effectively popularised Darwin's ideas. To heredity and biological factors Taine added the components of environment and immediate circumstances to complete a 'scientific' explanation of human behaviour in terms of 'race, moment et milieu'. With the growth of the 'scientific' method as promulgated by Renan, Taine and others in literature, man became an object to be observed, described and analysed in total neutrality. Man's behaviour was conceived of in machine-like terms; man stood outside the impulses of good or evil. Man could not be responsible for what he was or what he did since he was conditioned by forces beyond his control. This was the root cause of the furore over Naturalist doctrines. It was amorality more

‡See Bibliography: nos. *14* and *15*. J. Modave's promising 'Blasco Ibáñez et le naturalisme français', *Les Lettres Romanes*, 12 (1958), 287–301, unfortunately deals almost exclusively with *Sónnica la cortesana*.

than Darwinism that made Zola and his fellow naturalists the 'aesthetic pornographers' they were said to be. The common analogy of doctor and writer dissecting dispassionately the human body and mind (especially after the decisive influence on Zola of Claude Bernard's *Introduction a l'étude de la médecine expérimentale* [1865]) is, of course, fraught with difficulty as critics like McDowall and Martino* have shown. Able as he was to combine the 'tempérament' of the artist with impersonal scientific observation, Zola nevertheless interpreted the deterministic sciences in literary terms. Both the prologue to the second edition of *Thérèse Raquin* (1868) and *Le Roman expérimental* (1880) speak for "l'idée d'une littérature déterminée par la science", the scientific analogy being the key idea.

Let us examine Blasco Ibáñez's adaptation of these theories. One of the most striking features of the novel is the descriptions of the luxuriance and the forceful energy of nature and its effect on Barret and Batiste. Two critics have considered this problem in detail. V. A. Chamberlin's essay 'Las imágenes animalistas y el color rojo en *La barraca*' (*11*) is mainly concerned with stylistic usage and will be considered more fully in chapter VIII. However, his conclusion regarding the thematic use of the two images examined is helpful in this context.

> El hombre tiene una naturaleza doble, una alta faceta espiritual e intelectual, controlando otro aspecto latente, más primitivo y completamente animalista. Cualquier cosa que haga descomponer la faceta alta sirve para desencadenar la bestia dentro del hombre y producir su autodestrucción. Esto ocurre . . . a causa de la injusticia social, el alcohol, y los odios profundos . . . (*11*, 34-35).

Chamberlin correctly points to the consistent reiteration of animal images applied to Barret and the Borrulls in situations of stress and the colour red in situations of conflict, the two often overlapping. Yet this study only begins to tackle half the question. First Chamberlin implies that the 'normal' state is the "alta faceta

*A. McDowall, *Realism*, London, 1918; P. Martino, *Le Naturalisme français*, Paris, 1969. For a full account of the interest in physiology among French naturalists, see A. E. Carter, *The Ideas of Decadence in French Literature*, Toronto, 1958.

espiritual e intelectual". Secondly that it can be destroyed by
social injustice, alcohol and enmity. Rather it seems that the
emphasis is the other way about. Certainly man is brutalized by
the elements cited. The point is, however, that man is what Zola
termed a 'bête humaine'. Man is *a priori* a brute creature aspiring
to a "faceta alta". His inherent brutishness emerges under the
influence of social injustice, alcohol and enmity; they do not in
themselves drag him down to the level of the animal.

S. H. Eoff's study of *Cañas y barro* (*14*) is nearer the mark
when he argues that the Valencian novels are "the most thorough
adaptation of French Naturalism in Spain" (*14*, 115). Blasco
Ibáñez, he contends, discovered "a theme in perfect harmony
with the monistic foundations of naturalism". "Blasco Ibáñez . . .
assumes a monistic viewpoint and produces strong connecting
ties between the human being, his natural habitat, and the intellectual perspective that sees them as one" (*14*, 119). While *La
barraca* is not so thoroughly naturalistic in this sense as *Cañas y
barro* there are cogent reasons for supposing that *La barraca* was
a preparation for the latter. Zola's theories would have been
attractive to a lover of nature in the raw. They would also have
attracted a man whose nature was spontaneous and one who
liked physical adventure. Such a man, says Zamacois, one of his
earliest biographers, was Blasco Ibáñez*. "Moreover, he was not
restrained by religious convictions from plunging wholeheartedly
into the spirit of Zola's exaltation of primal natural forces"
(*14*, 116).

In effect, Blasco Ibáñez's portrait of the *huerta*, albeit at times
regionalist, also imparts the suggestion of a sinister primordial
power beyond the control of man but acting through him. The
opening paragraphs of the novel, as elsewhere, emphasise this
aspect. The "inmensa vega" wakens, yawns and stretches like
some slumbering giant. The menace of nature as it is aroused by
the dawn is implied in the vocabulary used : the nightingales
flee "como si les *hiriese* la luz del alba con sus reflejos de *acero*"
(25). The birds, like the children later (131), are "como un tropel
de pilluelos perseguidos, granujas". Amid the early morning

*E. Zamacois, *Mis contemporáneos. I*: *V. Blasco Ibáñez*, Madrid, 1910, pp.
22-26.

noises, those of animals dominate in contrast to the solitary hidden sacristans ringing their bells for mass (25). The scene is permeated with "un acre perfume de vegetación" as darkness is swallowed up by the furrows of the fields and the luxuriant foliage. Man, by contrast with the huge sweep of nature, is only one of a faceless "rosario de hormigas", an insignificant animal speck in the distance. As man and animal take up the burden of life they groan at the "rudo trabajo que pesaba sobre él apenas nacido el día". The accent is on heaviness, the slow and passive submission to toil, the trudging and mindless movement towards the city. Life penetrates forcibly into the sleeping *barracas* and the milch cows are vomited forth to the city. There, the anaemic Pepeta, tired out by ill-usage, hunger and overwork "con una paciencia de bestia sumisa esperaba que les diesen por las verduras el dinero que se había fijado" (27). There is the implication that man bows submissively before a power that weighs down and dominates him. Blasco Ibáñez is blending two levels of reality, the harsh earthiness of the *huerta* with its hot red sun and red soil and "a fateful overtone of transcendent implications" (*14*, 117). Within the milieu of the *huerta* he constructs a double tragedy, that of Barret and Batiste, the second essentially repeating that of the first. Man's pretensions are pitted in an unequal struggle against an all-powerful Nature that works its will through the medium of local conditions and through the innate brutality of the *huertanos*. Again and again Blasco Ibáñez evokes the feeling of a vague form of pessimistic pantheism. There is no evidence that he had even Zola's slight acquaintance with the works of Schopenhauer.* Nevertheless, a case could be argued to show that the deterministic theories of the German permeate the novels of both writers. Schopenhauer's theories embodied an impersonal kind of eternal unconscious in the world, which power manifested a strong animalistic cast. At base, nature is inimical to man. Nature's unconscious forces, controlling man at the instinctive and subrational level, overshadow his spiritual and

---

*See Eoff, *14*, 106, n. 41, who argues that (up to 1961) there was no evidence that Zola had read Schopenhauer. However, F. W. J. Hemmings does suggest some acquaintance with him: see *Emile Zola*, Oxford University Press, 2nd edition, 1966, pp. 182–83.

intellectual qualities and his pretensions to rational idealism. Man works in obedience to an endless irrational force (Schopenhauerian 'Will') and struggles for existence amid a nature that is constantly preying upon itself in a Darwinian process of life-and-death struggle for survival. The 'bête humaine' is inevitably involved in the struggle and becomes a sacrifice (see *14*, 92-93). One might argue that Blasco Ibáñez had thoroughly absorbed Zola's literary interpretation of these theories as he described Barret's final agonies before the eviction. "Barret . . . volvió con más ahinco a su trabajo, a matarse sobre aquellos terruños, que parecían crecer según disminuían sus fuerzas, envolviéndolo como un sudario rojo" (41). Words like "matarse", "crecer" and "sudario" underline the feeling of a superior power at work. The same is true of the description of "los campos del tío Barret" (32-33) with its "plantas parásitas", the "selva enana, enmarañada y deforme", "un oleaje de extraños tonos verdes . . . flores misteriosas y raras, de esas que sólo surgen en las ruinas y los cementerios". Under this 'jungle' there live and multiply "bichos asquerosos . . . largartos verdes de lomo rugoso, enormes escarabajos con caparazón de metálicos reflejos, arañas de patas cortas y vellosas, hasta culebras . . . Allí vivían . . . *devorándose unos a otros* . . ." The vegetation that engulfs the ruined *barraca* "era un sudario ocultando debajo de él centenares de cadáveres", "campo de muertes".

Barret is a victim of the forces of an all-powerful Nature and of heredity. The retrospective chapter II essentially repeats the larger narrative, the story of Batiste. At the outset we see Barret proudly maintaining the tradition of his forebears. Like them he has tamed a predatory Nature. Yet as the Barrets have tilled the land, the earth has bound them into its own struggle for survival. "No había uno que no estuviera regado con el sudor y la sangre de la familia" (37). The line goes back beyond the memory of the ancient Tomba. The victim of the forces of natural selection in an environment where physical strength is necessary to live, Barret has no sons and succumbs. "Fue este empeño una lucha sorda, desesperada, tenaz, contra las necesidades de la vida y contra su propia debilidad" (38). And so little by little he falls prey to more powerful forces in the "continua batalla con la tierra

y la miseria" (41). Batiste's struggle repeats that of Barret. "Fue
su vida una continua batalla" (57). By contrast with the barren-
ness of Sagunto the new lands pulse with fertile energy. "Siempre
verdes, con las entrañas incansables engendrando una cosecha tras
otra, circulando el agua roja a todas horas como vivificante sangre
por las innumerables acequias y regadoras que surcaban su super-
ficie como una complicada red de venas y arterías" (57-58).
Repeatedly the *huerta* is presented in terms of an animal, an
animal ready to devour, emphasising the unitary vision of nature,
animal and man bound together in the struggle for survival. It
has veins and arteries, it has "una espina erizada de púas que
eran sus canales" (66); "la vivificante sangre de la huerta" (75).
"Su tierra se resquebrajaba . . . formando mil bocas que en vano
esperaban un sorbo" (76); "sus trigos . . . formaban como un lago
de inquietas ondas" (121). The sun thrusts down "sus flechas de
oro" and its heat "hacía germinar la vida por todas partes" (142).
The choice of physiological terms, terms of pain, thirst, penetration and germination all point to the unitary and Naturalistic
vision of a struggle for existence where almost certain extinction
awaits the less improved forms of life. "The paramount intending
of nature, in a word, is concentrated upon the continuity and
improvement of the whole and not upon the individual" (*14*,
92). Man, bound to nature, succumbs in the unconscious forward
struggle. As the headless corpse of don Salvador topples into the
ditch his oneness with the animals is emphasised as his feet jerk
in "un pataleo fúnebre de res degollada" (50). Murderer and
victim are reduced to the brute, "una hiena" the one, "una bestia
herida" the other. As the latter is sacrificed nature devours un-
consciously and indifferently. As "las aguas se teñían de rojo",
the stream is seen "siguiendo su manso curso con un murmullo
plácido que alegraba el solemne silencio de la tarde" (50). With
the death of Barret "disolvióse su familia; desapareció como un
puñado de paja en el viento" (51). Ashes to ashes, dust to dust.
The stagnant water infects Pascualet so that at his funeral "la
vega, desperezándose voluptuosa . . . envolvía al muertecito con
su aliento oloroso . . . Los viejos árboles, que germinaban con una
savia de resurrección, parecían saludar al pequeño cadáver" (139).
Nature is already renewing itself in anticipation of the life it will

receive from death. The cyclic process of death giving way to life in the process of struggle forward is continually emphasised as when Batiste returns from hunting in the final chapter. Nature seems to swallow up man and "de las charcas surgió un hálito hediondo, la respiración venenosa de la fiebre palúdica" (165). The teeming germs and gases that claim Pascualet form a dominant motif from the "transpiración nocturna" (26) of chapter I onwards. Pimentó, mortally wounded, is bound to the soil like a snake as the earth sucks up his blood (169). Even Batiste has to struggle for survival from nature's maw as "se hundió en el barro". "Creyó morir, quedar enterrado en aquel lecho de fango" (169). Nature portrayed as a devouring monster suggests, especially in the heavy darkness of night, a power that decrees a sinister destiny for men. B. Hamel's study* examines naturalistic description in *Entre naranjos* and *Mare nostrum* in particular. The general conclusions are, however, directly relevant to this discussion.

> En su concepción naturalista de la vida, Blasco Ibáñez presenta las relaciones entre el hombre y la Naturaleza como una lucha sorda y feroz de la razón para sustraerse a las leyes naturales. En este eterno combate, el hombre se crea la ilusión de ser el centro del universo, cuando la triste verdad es que forma parte de la Naturaleza como un átomo insignificante, rodeado de un campo gravitatorio de fuerzas que lo arrastran en su movimiento. En el conflicto planteado, la Naturaleza, que tiene una función primordial que cumplir – la renovación de la vida con el concurso de la muerte –, se muestra por completo indiferente ante todas aquellas preocupaciones humanas que se separan del camino por ella trazado.

This type of Naturalistic vision will explain the predominance of natural description and the emphasis on physical detail. Such an emphasis cannot be explained in terms of *costumbrismo* alone.

There is hidden in the novel, however, a wider theme than that of human beings pitted against destructive natural forces, against "an all-powerful nature that works its will through the medium of local conditions" (*14*, 117). The novel is also a drama of man's

El paisaje en Blasco Ibáñez, unpublished doctoral thesis, University of Madrid, 1962.

frustrated attempt to rise above his natural condition, to transcend
'la bête humaine'. Man, as Chamberlin has argued, is spiritual
and brutal, that is, rational or subconsciously instinctive. Man is
also self-conscious or mass-conscious. As peasants Barret and
Batiste are a part of a species bound to the earth. This is emphasised by the accent on physicality. On the other level, as
fathers and individuals they manifest traces of rational refine-
ment. While the determinist vision offers the picture of earth-
bound figures toiling in obedience to forces beyond their control
(as the author would have seen in Zola's *La Terre*), as individuals
they manifest higher traits: love, family loyalty, fidelity to mate,
grief and at special moments a sense of sympathy, understanding
and tolerance. Such is their reaction after the death of Pascualet.
As a group the peasants march mechanically and instinctively to
the city at dawn to return at nightfall in an unbroken daily
round. Teresa's journey, like Roseta's, describes an unending
cycle of repetitious action, a passive sluggish ant-like movement
in obedience to a superior power. When moved to anger they
react instinctively to return to the animal in an orgy of violence
and destruction. Barret on eviction and Batiste after Pascualet's
death behave in this fashion. The *huertanos* at casa de Copa and
after Pimento's death similarly resort to brute force. Even the
"mansedumbre" of Barret and his fellows before the eviction,
their individual mental adjustment to a situation beyond their
control, is a form of collective passivity from which only under
extreme provocation are they aroused to "cierto instinto de rebelión" (42). The reaction of the mob to Barret's tragedy is similar
to that of Zola's mobs. Individual personality is rapidly devoured
by mass consciousness and rational feelings evaporate. Both
Barret and Batiste, usually calm and patient men, break out,
under the pressures of nature's devouring power and social injustice, with homicidal rage. "El pobre viejo parecía loco" (46);
"continuaba rugiendo en su cabeza el ansia de la destrucción"
(47); "era terrible el aspecto de aquel hombretón siempre tranquilo y cachazudo. Despertaba la fiera en él, cansado de que lo
hostigasen un día y otro día. En sus ojos inyectados de sangre
brillaba la fiebre del asesinato; todo su cuerpo se estremecía de
cólera, esa terrible cólera del pacífico" (125). The use of terms of

animality, blood, extreme emotion underscores the point that the author is making.

Unlike Zola, Blasco Ibáñez shows little interest in the notion of individual heredity. Barret, it is true, inherits from his forebears a love of the soil and their obedience to its call. "El amor de sus amores, eran aquellas tierras, sobre las cuales había pasado monótona y silenciosa la historia de su familia" (37). Batiste, once miller and carter, is atavistic in his love for the soil. This emerges unequivocally in the clearing of the overgrown fields in chapter III. The accent in this novel, however, is more on heredity as a general force linking the *huertanos* with their distant past, the age of the Moorish domination of the province. While there is no specific mention of any theory of evolution or heredity, given the persistent references to "una gente que lleva en sus venas sangre moruna" (26) it seems very likely that Blasco Ibáñez was attempting to incorporate into *La barraca* something of the great power of the hereditary principle he would have found in Naturalist literature. This aspect is, though, one of the least successful aspects of the novel. The references are sporadic and do not add up to a specific statement of a principle at work. It may be that the first version, *Venganza moruna*, contained a consistent and well-integrated theme along these lines that, when expanded, was lost. Vázquez Cey's impressionistic

> Moriscos los hombres, morisco el paisaje y morisco también el entero movimiento psicológico y moral de la obra . . . salmo fatalista que condena las criaturas al aniquilamiento, especie de soplo de simún entre cuyas espirales la voluntad se pulveriza*

overstresses Koranic fatality. L. Tailhade's whimsical 'Est-ce vraiment une survivance orientale?'† is even less helpful. The important factor is that the theme is inconsistent and clumsy. The last sentence of chapter I provides one example. Emphasising the broad perspective of time linking the *huertano* with his distant past, the era of the Moors, the author recreates the sense of alarm

---

*'*La barraca*, novela mediterránea', *Humanidades* (Argentina), 24 (1934), 306
†Tailhade, 8.

at the approach of Moorish pirates seeking Christian slaves (36). Another example is Batiste, at one moment an Aragonese, at another facing life with Moorish resignation. It is true that the Moorish characteristics of the peasantry are stressed. Their "gravedad" (43), "ciega bravura" (44), "pasión africana" (80), "previsión" (125), "impasividad" (135), "postura" (139), "cariño" (163), "resignación" (180) are all attributed to a people who are characterised as direct descendants of the Moors. The people squat like Moors (133), mount their horses (121) and teach their children (99) in Moorish fashion; they share the same love of beauty and water (94) and of the soil (163). They offer a historical parallel with their Moorish ancestors: the Moors are evicted as are Barret and Batiste. The *huerta* is bathed in "un sol africano" (142) and the "cauce del Turia" seems "un desierto africano" (116). Yet all this detail has little effect on the shaping of the story. The references offer a decorative motif rather than a specific theory of given factors explaining certain effects. Only crudely does the theme account for the explosion of rage in passive personalities.

In Zola the retrogressive perspective of man's heredity, especially animal sexuality, is a conspicuous theme. In *La Terre*, *Germinal, La Bête humaine*, sex is as pervasive a theme as the image of the power of the soil, the mine or the railway engine. Such is not the case in *La barraca*. Nowhere is there depicted a scene as in *La Terre* where man and beast act out in unison the process of procreation and birth. Indeed, in this novel, Blasco Ibáñez is less frank than Pardo Bazán's prudish *Los pazos de Ulloa*. Pepeta's anaemia and gynaecological ailment (28) or the seedy dens of prostitution in the barrio de Pescadores (29) are dismissed with none of the raw realism of a Zola. The conversation between Pepeta and Rosario calls forth no examination of the adventures of a prostitute. Peasant modesty causes Rosario a feeling of shame despite her coarsening experiences. There is no sense of the spontaneous and energetic animal sexuality of Zola's peasants, only a stress on social injustice. Compared with the equation of sexual need to hunger at the rendezvous in *Germinal*, the casual, brutal possession in *La Terre* or the "silent and brutal" embraces of *Thérèse Raquin* the *huertanos* are exceedingly chaste

At the silk factory the girls, unlike Catherine and Chaval in *Germinal*, amuse themselves "hostilizando a los hombres con miradas insolentes para que les dijesen algo y chillar después falsamente escandalizadas, emprendiendo con ellos un tiroteo de desvergüenzas" (83). They may discuss "cosas internas" (95) but there is no improper behaviour. Roseta and Tonet's relationship is 'innocent'. "Jamás asomó entre ellos el punzante deseo, la audacia de la carne" (93). Nor is there any real accent on the coarseness of other physiological processes : the little boy defecating in fear (103) or the death agonies of Pascualet or Pimentó. Compare the account of the child's death (123) with, say, the death of Mouche (*La Terre*), of Coupeau (*L'Assommoir*) or the horrifying agonies of Emma Bovary. K. Reding's assertion that Blasco Ibáñez "is naturalistic to the extent of employing these (regional) specific terms . . . but the coarse colloquialisms, never"* is true. There is only one coarse expletive (36) and a few instances of strong abuse. As with his contemporaries, Galdós, Alas, Pardo Bazán and Palacio Valdés, so for the Valencian the demands of scientific exactitude threw up a number of bizarre novelistic problems. The ultimate was that before which all of them, including Blasco Ibáñez, retreated : the question of the slice-of-life. Torrente Ballester's intemperate comment that the novels smell of "sudor" and "sexo" is certainly inapplicable to *La barraca*. K. Reding is nearer the mark when she observes that the scenes "make us shudder, but our sense of propriety is not outraged."† If sex does appear it is subordinated to a vague but powerful urge to live. Even in the face of death from hunger in Sagunto, Batiste's instinct for survival through offspring triumphs. Birth and death are at the service of the Schopenhauerian vision of an all-powerful nature, Will; the individual instinctively behaves in a manner that ensures the continuity of unending creation whatever his rational convictions (see *14*, 106). This popular version of Schopenhauer as adapted by Zola is hinted at in the account of the growth of Batiste's family (56) who later assume the aspect of a force that threatens to devour the parents (77-78).

*K. Reding, 367.
†*Ibid.*, 367.

Like Zola, Blasco Ibáñez seems to adumbrate an "abstract life principle, unindividuated, which governs all, including the death of individuals" (*41*, 107). The author is not so much interested in character as in situation. Human beings are pitted against nature. While other social factors explain in some degree the tragedies of Barret and Batiste, to a large extent they are secondary to the stronger ones of instinct and basic sexuality "which operate at the bidding of an all-powerful Nature that works its will through the medium of local conditions" (*14*, 117). Chamberlin's assumption that

> Para el explosivo huertano el problema de controlarse es harto difícil. Estimulándose el aspecto animalista de su naturaleza, hay fuerzas poderosas según Blasco: el clima . . . el suelo, consideraciones etnológicas (feroz sangre moruna) y – especialmente – explotación económica (*11*, 35)

approaches the problem from the wrong side. Blasco Ibáñez is not so much interested in the dynamics of the man. His attention is drawn to the end-product, the effect wrought by the shaping power of heredity and environment. Given the nature of man's milieu he cannot be other than he is.

Blasco Ibáñez's presentation of a deterministic vision may at times be diffuse or inconsistent but its presence cannot be denied. C. Barja seems to have sensed this when he suggested that the author instinctively felt rather than thought out a philosophy (*5*, 393), that he lived life rather than pondered on it. This view is underlined by the biography of Zamacois. This explains in some measure the lack of rigour and cohesion over certain aspects of determinist theory. If anything Blasco Ibáñez's world depends on even more basic stimuli. The "dos apremiantes necesidades", argues Barja, are "la necesidad material de subsistir, el hambre; y la necesidad también material de sobrevivir, el sexo. Hambre y sexo: por allí empieza la filosofía de Blasco Ibáñez. Es un dominante sentido materialista de la vida" (*5*, 393).

Gómez de Baquero's comment in *La Gaceta Literaria* in November 1927 that "La influencia de Zola en España se debió más a la moda o, si se quiere, a la actualidad literaria, que a las relativas afinidades entre el realismo español y el naturalismo francés" is, of course, as incorrect as J. Cassou's judgement that "tandis que les romans de Zola produisent un effet de pessimisme morose et appliqué, ceux de Blasco paraissent entraînants et ensoleillés"* or N. González Ruiz's estimate that *La barraca* "se defiende . . . de los ataques del microbio naturalista".† It is the pessimistic earthbound materialism described above rather than adventitious coincidences of style and technique that should argue for a critical claim to see Blasco Ibáñez as 'a Spanish Zola'.

*J. Cassou, *La Littérature espagnole*, Paris, 1929, p.115.
†N. González Ruiz, *En esta hora*, Madrid, 1925, p.172.

5 La barraca *and naturalism: the power of the bourgeoisie*

In 1909 A. González Blanco noted that *La barraca* "es la novela más perfecta de Blasco Ibáñez . . . en ella se esboza por vez primera las preocupaciones de los problemas sociales" (*6*, 592-93). Sixty years later Betoret Paris sharpened the focus and lamented the fact that the Valencian novels were still not accepted as a serious attempt to interpret a socio-political theme in literary terms. Glossing E. Sebastià (*13*), Betoret Paris observed that "Las coordenadas históricas de 1848 y del Segundo Imperio francés corresponden en España a la crisis de 1873 y a la Restauración, y su intérprete fue Blasco Ibáñez; pero que a diferencia de Zola no ha sido comprendido todavía ni estudiado a fondo".* Apart from Sebastià's study the majority of interpretations along socio-political lines have scarcely risen above the superficial. Torrente Ballester's comments, quoted in chapter I, are a case in point. In 1967, however, V. Ribelles Pérez (*8*) and J. León Roca (*12*) drew attention to the strongly Republican commitment of Blasco Ibáñez, the reaction in Spain to the *affaire Dreyfus* and his organization of a letter of solidarity to the condemned Zola from the citizens of Valencia. Since then, in 1971, R. Pérez de la Dehesa has uncovered a considerable corpus of evidence to suggest that Zola, for a number of Spanish writers, was much more than a literary figure. His essay (*15*) is important in that it shows how Zola served Spanish liberals as a spearhead for the short-lived attack on the bourgeois politics of accommodation and for the liberal attempt to drag Spain from the *marasmo intelectual* of the last decades of the century. Zola's works in translation were published cheaply in large numbers with the idea, as Blasco Ibáñez

*'El caso Blasco Ibáñez', *Hispania* (U.S.A.), 52 (1969), 99. See note on p. 10 above. For the historical background in France, see: D. W. Brogan,*The Development of Modern France, 1870-1933*, London, 1940; *The French Nation (1814-1940)*, London, 1957; J. M. Thompson, *Louis Napoleon and the Second Empire*, Oxford, 1954; H. Tint, *Modern France*, London, 1966 (a useful digest); A. Cobban, *A History of Modern France*, Harmondsworth, 1962.

explained in a letter to Zola, "que le peuple espagnol s'illustre". Alongside Zola the works of Kropotkin and other left-wing writers were also issued in cheap format. Blasco Ibáñez and his liberal acquaintances saw Zola as a revolutionary saint, an evangelist whose novels would arouse, through their educational potential, a similar potential for social and political regeneration.

This aspect of the impact of Zola is as important as the pessimistic and materialist strain of Naturalist thought just examined. Indeed, both aspects belong to that simple underlying idea that conditioned the thought of Blasco Ibáñez and his contemporaries: that human life cannot be represented in a fully meaningful or truthful manner without taking account of the pressures brought to bear upon the individual by the particularity of social situation and historical circumstances – Taine's much popularised 'race, moment et milieu'. Unlike Pereda and the other *costumbristas*, as we have seen, Blasco Ibáñez discusses specific social problems. His early novels, argues Blanco Aguinaga, "nos dan: (a) un análisis realista crítico de los conflictos sociales . . . y (b) una interpretación progresista de esos conflictos" (*10*, 192). E. Sebastià sees the Valencian novels as specifically 'Naturalist' within the terms of Arnold Hauser's *The Social History of Art* (London, 1951). *La barraca* as a *folletín* novel, suggests Sebastià, marks a part of a process, gaining ground in the last decades of the nineteenth century, whereby literature was being disseminated over a wider social milieu. Hitherto the leisured upper and middle classes had formed, in general, the exclusive clientele of the novelist and essayist. Indeed, many of the bourgeoisie regarded access to literature as their exclusive patrimony, the hallmark of their social status and wealth (*13*, 27). The newspaper serial-novel was to break that exclusivism. *La barraca* is meant for the masses. Accepting Hauser, he argues that Naturalism is, in brief, an art of opposition and an expression of the will to social regeneration. His thesis demonstrates how Valencia provided an ideal climate for the development of a genuine form of 'Hauserian' Naturalism in Spain. Valencia and the French Second Empire, according to Sebastià, sharing a common socio-economic and political situation, provided a common ethos in which Zola's and Blasco Ibáñez's literary interpretations of the

world were developed. Sebastià suggests that under the growing
bourgeoisie of the 1870s the *huertano* became a "proletari alienat"
(*13*, 51). Isolated on the *huerta* in the control of *caciques* (see *16*,
366ff) and the victim of bourgeois provincial protectionism, the
peasant shared hardly any of the benefits of industrial progress.
This perpetuated traditional work-patterns, respect for property
and the sense of dependence on the land-owning classes (*13*, 36,
16, 343 & *17*). With the drought and the economic crisis of 1884-
85 the unskilled peasant held a poor bargaining position. The
family group came to rely on a pattern of subsidiary employments
that forced the *huertanos* to a greater dependence on the capital
(*13*, 62). The sale of vegetables and melons, of milk, the silk and
tobacco factories, shop employment and domestic service are the
fate of the peasants as they are of Pepeta, Roseta, Tonet and
Rosario in the novel. The worker becomes enslaved on the land
and is further exploited by tolls, and during the slump, higher
rents (*13*, 62-3). Barret and Pepeta are the novelistic victims of
this aspect of the economy. The situation was aggravated, as we
have seen, by the large-scale immigration of displaced Aragonese
who threatened the employment of the *huertanos* (*13*, 110). The
threat of hunger, the crippling burden of work and the constant
fear of eviction turns peasant passivity into violence. The culmination is the 'huelga de los colonos' reported by *Las Provincias*
in 1880 (see above, chapter III). This is the socio-economic background to the novel. On the one side we have the tragic figure of
Barret, victim of the system. On the other the enemies of the
workers, Don Salvador's heirs and Doña Matilde, living in cool
aloofness at a comfortable distance from the workers' huts. There
is also the instrument of their justice, the Civil Guard, who patrol
the *huerta* and enforce the laws of the bourgeoisie. "A socio-
economic problem" observed Sebastià, "that neither boundary
guards, rural police nor the Civil Guard were able to resolve. *La
barraca* . . . is nothing more than the chronicle of the tense
relationships between the tenants and the owners who live in the
city" (*13*, 54). Law and order could be maintained but the social
problem that caused disorder remained unsolved. Raymond Carr
has commented on the ease with which the monarchist restoration was accomplished and socialism sternly controlled (*16*, 342).

By the mid-70s the privileged classes with their domination of the bureaucracy, parliament (through the *caciques*), and the Civil Guard, and with their financial and journalistic strength, no longer feared for social peace. The socialism of the Revolution of 1868 had been a political failure; it could provide no guarantees for order and stability. "It was the collapse of the forces of public order and not a collapse in economic prosperity which embarrassed governments. . . . As long as the moral atmosphere was dominated by the fear of a relapse into political chaos and social revolution, the institutions of constitutional monarchy remained inviolable for all but Republicans and Carlists" (*16*, 343 & 345). In a situation like this the peasant suffered economically with little room for political dissent. It is small wonder that Pimentó's *huertanos* hold on so tenaciously to the little gains they have made.

It will be clear by now that *La barraca* is concerned with this problem. The novel is rich enough in suggestiveness to admit of various interpretations. One of the most obvious is a picture of a peculiar set of socio-economic conditions which emphasises the insecurity of land-tenure and the injustice and exploitation suffered by the workers. The difficulty lies in isolating exactly what specific theories Blasco Ibáñez develops in the novel. It may be that the paucity of studies in this area can partly be explained by the fact that Blasco Ibáñez's liberalism is diffuse and, at times, contradictory.

The opening chapter, as we have seen, depicts man in his relations to the world of nature. On another level nature, the *huerta*, is also presented as a monstrous instrument in the hands of an indifferent, anonymous power, the landowners. The first part of the novel dwells in considerable detail on the lot of the peasant and tells the story of the misfortunes of two particular individuals, the emphasis being on hard physical labour. As dawn breaks the peasants move in faceless ranks ant-like to their work. Attention is focused on one figure, the anaemic Pepeta. Rising at three, on arrival at the city she cannot even afford a warming coffee against the cold and, a "bestia sumisa", waits to bargain with the merchants. The bargaining complete, she immediately returns, as Sebastià has indicated, "para desarrollar una segunda industria :

después de las hortalizas, la leche" (27). Alongside her stride "la virginidad de la huerta", the silk and tobacco girls hardened and insensible "a este despertar que presenciaba diariamente" (28), "una avalancha de gente laboriosa". At the city limits Pepeta is forced to pay over some of her hard-won money at the unjust "fielato de consumos" (29). Roseta, later, joins this double journey, at dawn and at nightfall, and spends the interim in the steamy rooms of the silk factory. The repetitive, inexorable round of daily toil is stressed. The crushing burden of work has deprived the *huertanos* of any higher feelings or aspirations. Like patient beasts they awaken and with their animals move mindlessly off to Valencia. There they will earn just enough to keep themselves alive for the next day's work.

In the previous chapter it was argued that Blasco Ibáñez's attempt to portray the hereditary principle of Moorish ancestry in the *huertanos* was inconsistent. Yet the persistent references to a fatalistic view of life underscored by the double "resignación oriental" and "la pasividad del fatalismo" (180) in the concluding paragraph of the novel should not be lightly dismissed. Carr has observed that because the peasant "did not see the social war as a long struggle but as a sudden triumph of the truths learned from itinerant apostles and the primitive press, he failed to organize . . . Once the prospect of land had vanished, millenarianism . . . remained only in the hearts of *fanáticos*: thus is explained the cyclical nature of rural anarchism so brilliantly described by Díaz del Moral [see note on page 10], the sudden relapse into 'Moorish' fatalism, apathy, and brute indifference" (*16*, 444-45). As the militant anarchist, Mella, once noted, "the peasantry are quick to understand and enthuse, quick to surrender and despair". An explanation of the theme of 'resignation' and 'fatalism' along these lines may prove more satisfactory than an interpretation in terms of Naturalistic principles of heredity.

In Valencia Pepeta meets Rosario, once honourable, now descended to prostitute and maid of all work. At this poignant episode the theme of the boycott is introduced, the bare details of what is to be expanded in chapter II. "De todo tenía la culpa el amo de la tierra, aquel don Salvador, . . . ¡Ah, ladrón! . . . ¡Y cómo había perdido a toda una familia!" (31). Capitalist greed has caused unwarranted human misery. As the story develops so the repercussions of don Salvador's avarice spread outwards to engulf further victims, the Borrulls, and finally cause the deaths of their child and Pimentó. Even then this legacy of bitterness is not exhausted, for one supposes that the effects will fall on other innocents who come after. In chapter II the central figures are portrayed in unequivocal terms: the honourable, hard-working Barret, "hombre animoso, de costumbres puras" (38) and don Salvador, "viejo avaro" of "fama detestable" (39), dressed in tatters, the object of the hostility and fear of the *huerta* and the alarums of the dogs. We cannot doubt the author's sympathies. While Pimentó is all for violence (39) we know the *huertanos* cannot win. Don Salvador and his associates are too powerful. They control the law and the forces of public order; "con gente así siempre pierde el pobre" (40). Barret is a victim of nature and usury. He loses his horse and the "voraz usurero" helps him out of difficulty. The heavy irony here, especially in the passage that begins "Pero la Providencia . . ." (41) indicates the authorial viewpoint. It is a deliberately ironic misuse of the type of statement used by novelists like Pereda and Alarcón. Barret is forced into the triple burden of the struggle with nature, the rental and the exorbitant interest on the loan. His reaction is predictable enough. "Estas angustias . . . acabaron por despertar en él cierto instinto de rebelión. . . . ¿Por qué no eran suyos los campos?" Generations of his family had worked the fields to make the barren fertile. "Y ahora venía a apretarle la argolla, a hacerle morir con sus recordatorios, aquel viejo sin entrañas que era el amo, aunque no sabía coger un azadón ni en su vida había doblegado el espinazo . . . ¡Cristo! ¡Y cómo arreglan las cosas los hombres!" (42). But for all these revolutionary sentiments Barret quickly returns to "el respeto tradicional y supersticioso para la propiedad. Había que trabajar y ser honrado" (42). The loaded "supersticioso", like the presentation of an apparent *costumbrismo*, implies that the peasant mentality has been formed in an ethos that plays on his lack of education and narrow horizons, his fear of authority and the illusion of progress. Only on eviction does Barret revolt in an orgy of destruction and murder. No blame is imputed; indeed, the *huertanos* close ranks in solidarity and a conspiracy of silence.

The old man is shielded from the law, "enredos de los hombres para perder a las gentes de bien" (43-4). The author is emphasising that the landowners intrigue with the lawgivers against the just causes of the peasantry. As Carr has observed, "patronage had always conditioned justice" (*16*, 372).

J. Devlin has suggested that the Tribunal "shows the social system at its worst".* In the face of calumny Batiste is enraged and commits contempt. He feels the justice of his cause and cannot understand that the word of an honest man is insufficient for the syndics, "todas buenas personas" (71). The court, formerly praised, becomes of a sudden "el monstruo de las siete cabezas", ready to devour. He now understands why social injustice causes man to murder man as Barret had done before him (72). In the long description of the Tribunal the antiquity of the institution is emphasised by the terms used: "cinco siglos, cincuenta años, viejo, carcomido por los siglos, desfigurados, maltrechos, roídos, rotas" (66). Is Blasco Ibáñez associating the decay of the Church with the injustice of the Tribunal held in its shadow? Has the Church allied itself with the system to exploit the worker? Apart from the bells (25), Teresa's churchgoing and this reference, the Church hardly appears in the novel. It offers little or no pastoral comfort. The *albaet*, of course, is more primitive ritual than Christian burial. Yet suddenly the sympathies shift uneasily when we learn that the *huertanos* are masters of their own justice. "Mostrábanse orgullosos los huertanos de su tribunal. Aquello era hacer justicia; la pena sentenciada inmediatamente, y nada de papeles, pues estos sólo sirven para enredar a los hombres honrados" (68). Where does the author stand? Blasco Ibáñez may be underlining the justice and rightness of the system. He is also calling attention to the frailty of man in operating such a system.

The ambiguity here is paralleled by the story at large. L. B. Kiddle has noted that "The presentation is somewhat confusing since the author awakens our sympathy for the tenant farmer in the tragic struggle of tío Barret only to swing our allegiance over to Batiste as he stands alone against the prejudiced, tradition-

Spanish Anticlericalism, New York, 1966, p.97.

bound farmers"*. This might be counted the major flaw of the novel. Given Blasco Ibáñez's political views at this time, and the influences of his revolutionary mentors, Bark, Sawa, Asensi and Ruiz Zorrilla†, there is a failure to be consistently radical. As a critic of absentee landlords and exploitation he must sympathise with Barret and the *huertanos*. This he does. The difficulty arises when his hero breaks the boycott. Batiste immediately incurs a natural hostility as a 'blackleg'. He is a tool of the capitalists in the unsophisticated political thinking of the workers. At the same time Batiste is the prototype for the worker-heroes of the thesis novels of the early 1900s. His heroic revolt against the law of the *riego* in an assertion of 'natural' justice anticipates the actions of the worker-heroes of the series that began with *La catedral* (1903). The theme is the same: "desesperado héroe de la lucha por la vida, guardando los suyos" (79). This idealistic notion of just men acting out their own instinctive justice is consistently stressed. The peasant works the land; it is he who must control it, he who must resolve the conflicts. After the fight with Pimentó he looks for no legal action from the city; it is peasant vengeance he fears. "¿Para qué necesitaba un hombre jueces ni Guardia Civil, teniendo buen ojo y una escopeta en su barraca? Las cosas de los hombres deben resolverlas los hombres mismos" (163). Despite their enmity towards Batiste the *huertanos* do not betray him to the bourgeoisie. This notion of 'natural justice', reminiscent of the theories of Savigny‡, is, of course, false. There is no guarantee that a truly anarchist concept of a system of justice built on individual conscience or observed custom would prove any more beneficial or just than the codified system of laws of the capitalists in Valencia. Indeed, the lie is given to Blasco Ibáñez's Anarchist Utopianism by the 'justice' that Pimentó takes

*Introduction to *La barraca*, New York, 1960, p.xv.

†C. Pitollet, 'A propos de Blasco Ibáñez', *Bulletin Hispanique*, 30 (1928), 235–36 and J. Just Gimeno, *Blasco Ibáñez i València*, Valencia, 1931, p.35.

‡Savigny, a German jurist, was widely influential among liberal reformers in Catalonia as well as among *institucionistas* like Giner de los Ríos. Blasco Ibáñez may have come across the theories of Savigny during his friendship with the Federalist Pi y Margall. Savigny viewed law as a slow, almost imperceptible growth, like language. "Law is first developed", wrote Savigny, "by custom and popular faith, next by judicial decisions—everywhere, therefore, by internal silently operating powers, not by the arbitrary will of a law-giver."

into his own hands. In the same way, whatever the provocations and hardships endured by Barret, no system of justice, natural or capitalist, can condone murder. If Blasco Ibáñez was, in the words of his political mentor, Pi y Margall, "un federalista intransigente" who believed in the International† as a potent force for revolution from below, if Blasco Ibáñez had as extraordinary a grasp on political theory and history as his *Historia de la revolución española* (1890-1892) would suggest (*10*, 196ff.), the reader cannot but be confused and disappointed at the woolly thinking of the socio-politics of *La barraca*. Blasco Ibáñez clearly admires primitive, 'natural' patterns of social organisation untainted by the interests and economics of the capital. It could be argued that he had also been influenced by Joaquín Costa's theory that social structures are repositories of concepts like justice just as institutions are ethnic fossils of social attitudes and law.‡ The author admires worker solidarity, a theme stressed from the outset. He also respects the law of the gun, a law he himself used in his South-American 'colonies' in 1910 when faced with a mutiny of discontented immigrants. The confusion emerges when allegiance is transferred from the *huertanos* to the hero. One might argue here that since the naturalist novel should be an impersonal account of observed reality, the novelist is attempting to present the evidence impartially. He sympathises with the workers, he also sympathises with Batiste. The difficulty emerges when Blasco Ibáñez attempts to extract political capital from the confrontation.

Batiste's Aragonese energy affronts the neighbourhood (61-2); the parochialism of the *huerta* rejects the family when the boycott is broken, provoking "un estremecimiento de alarma, de extrañeza, de indignación" (36). Finally, the Borrulls are hated because they are outsiders. Worker conspires against worker but not totally at the behest of the landlords. Batiste is the victim of the clash between two rights. The right to work, to earn a living

†The First International Working Men's Association, held in 1864, was the earliest successful attempt at international revolutionary association. Formed under the theoretical and organizational guidance of Marx and Engels, its revolutionary enthusiasm did much to stimulate the emergence and growth of Socialist labour organization in Spain.

‡Costa, *La poesía popular. Mitología y literatura celtohispana*, Madrid, 1881.

and feed the family is at odds with the natural rights of the *huerta* collective to work its land unexploited and feed itself, free from the predatory absentee landowners. This particularly Hegelian notion of tragedy was widely discussed in intellectual circles in the 1880s and 1890s, not least by González Serrano, an acquaintance of Blasco Ibáñez*.

We might also explain the ambiguity in those terms set out in the introductory chapter. Blasco Ibáñez may be exploring the means whereby a man can come to terms with reality. Batiste, a worker of idealism and energy, is undone by forces beyond his control. He successfully overcomes a natural force that had undone his predecessor, he allies himself with the economic interests that had evicted his predecessor, but, unlike Barret, collides headlong with an implicit class-hatred (albeit he, though an outsider, is still a worker) and explicit parochialism and superstition. Wherein lies the root of the tragedy? The Valencian entrepreneurs? The peasants? The sinister forces of the *huerta*? Batiste's stubborn pride? Or his devotion to his family? Perhaps the 'reality' of the situation is a combination of all these components. Indeed, this richness of suggestivity may be the key to why the novel has enjoyed such a continued success. In the final analysis it could be argued that the author is more interested in his worker hero and his struggle forward than he is in condemning the socio-economics of the capitalist system. If any conclusion does emerge clearly it must be that of man's inhumanity to man.

Then there is the question of the ending of the novel. It, too, is ambiguous. According to Cheyne, "in Batiste's determination to continue the struggle lies the essence of Blasco Ibáñez's optimism. *La barraca* is a novel of protest, not of hopelessness"†. Kiddle interprets the novel in like fashion:

> The final defeat of Batiste should not be interpreted as proof of the pessimism of the author. Blasco is pessimistic about the role that society and its traditions play in thwarting the individ-

---

* See S. H. Eoff, *The Novels of Pérez Galdós*, St. Louis, 1954, chapter VII; idem, *The Modern Spanish Novel*, New York, 1961. See also A. C. Bradley, *Oxford Lectures on Poetry*, London, 1955, pp. 69–98.

†G. Cheyne (ed), *La barraca*, London, 1964, p.18.

ual, but he is optimistic about the capacity for courageous struggle found in a human being (xv).

But the issue is not so clear-cut. For all his energy Batiste has lost. This is not the first time his efforts have come to naught. Batiste's pre-history "era un continuo cambio de profesión, siempre dentro del círculo de la miseria rural, mudando cada año de oficio, sin encontrar para su familia el bienestar mezquino que constituía toda su aspiración" (56). As miller's boy, as carter, as farmer in Sagunto and as *huertano* "la mala suerte le perseguía" (56). The family depart from the novel as they entered it, with nothing. All their energies have been in vain. The point is underlined by the repetition of a key phrase. In chapter I as Pepeta watches the pathetic spectacle of the Borrulls, they are described as "oliendo a hambre, a fuga desesperada, como si la desgracia marchase tras de la familia pisándole los talones" (35). In casa de Copa Pimentó's threat "¡Vesten o te mate!" means another eviction "llevando como tétrica escolta la fea hambre, que iría pisándole los talones" (159). When that momentary vision becomes an actuality in the final chapter, the family face the prospect of flight again. "Huirían de allí . . . sintiendo el hambre detrás de ellos pisándoles los talones" (179). The cyclic nature of Batiste's fortunes is underlined by a repetition that can hardly be coincidental. In a situation where man is the victim of man's irrational hate and man's greed brings death and tragedy, where life is "una batalla implacable", there can be little hope. Batiste may stride off into the new dawn "para empezar otra vida" but his springing tread would be as much the result of escape as of optimism.

We cannot doubt the author's sympathy and righteous indignation. There does seem, however, to be a genuine conflict between his radical and his scientific aspirations as well as between these and his instinctive sympathies. The Naturalist doctrine led him to see men as products, as the end of a process rather than the whole process itself. One of the defects of Naturalist literary technique is, in the words of Sebastià, "the limitations produced by the predominance of a static vision of society to the detriment of a really dynamic vision" (*13*, 32). In *La barraca*, as in other naturalist novels, the demand for an absolute exactitude makes it difficult for the author, if he intended to, to introduce a really

dynamic and autonomous hero into the scheme or to suggest
ways, through him, in which ideas and actions might affect the
course of history. Batiste is certainly idealistic but he never
becomes a dynamic personality. First his horizons are too narrow;
his interests are focused solely on his family and not on the class-
struggle. Secondly he is used as a kind of operator whose portrait
is of less interest than the actions he instigates. It is here that the
embryonic radical thesis is at odds with the determinist theories
of Naturalism. In the same way the technique of objective documentation is also at variance with the author's evident sympathies,
first with the workers and, subsequently, to the detriment of the
workers, with Batiste. If he supports worker solidarity and industrial action, the boycott, he cannot sympathise with both the
huertanos and Batiste. While both are exploited from outside the
huerta such a split allegiance seriously weakens the force of the
socio-political thesis. The story becomes a simple human tragedy
where man's aspirations and energies come to naught through
a given set of factors whose influence cannot be avoided. Tragedy
is unavoidable in a deterministic world.

La barraca, then, could be interpreted as a novel of defeat.
Blasco Ibáñez has asserted the limitations, natural and social,
under which his character acts and postpones questions of responsibility and progress. Blasco Ibáñez's would-be Marxism breaks
down when he denies the existence of any genuinely dynamic
elements in society. He portrays with detachment and ultimately
with complacency puny, tied men against a realistic backdrop.
His world is static, pessimistically conceived, deterministic in the
least constructive sense. He is certainly not calumniating the
worker (of which Zola had been accused). However, we cannot
leave aside one purely moral objection. Even though in real life
there are social situations so extreme that moral judgements
become nonsense, their depiction in literature is not particularly
edifying.

On the other hand there is a hint of a belief in education as a
means to moral and social progress. Don Joaquín is its spokes-
man. The description of the schoolroom near the molino de la
Cadena (99) reflects the lowly level of instruction received. The
lack of light symbolises the lack of intellectual illumination. The

schoolmaster himself has few pretensions to learning: he has travelled, been an engine-driver, knows herbal remedies, can read and write and has a few social graces. His pitiable sense of superiority is nourished by the uncritical and parrot-like interjections of his wife. His claim to distinction relies on the above 'education' and his esoteric attire (136). This man is the mouthpiece for progressive ideas. On the two occasions that he appears, don Joaquín remarks that the *huertanos* are "bestias, brutos . . ." (100).

> En el fondo son buena gente. Muy brutos, eso sí, capaces de las mayores barbaridades, pero con un corazón que se conmueve ante el infortunio y les hace ocultar las garras . . . ¡Pobre gente! ¿Qué culpa tienen si nacieron para vivir como bestias y nadie les saca de su condición? . . . Aquí lo que se necesita es instrucción, mucha instrucción (137).

Expressed by so humorous a figure in so humble a place, the effect is ambiguous. Is the author pessimistic about the realisation of these dreams of "mucha instrucción"? If pessimistic, who is to blame? Only indirectly must we suppose that it is the landowners themselves who keep the workers enslaved by a lack of education. They maintain their control by a combination of charity and jobbery; they divert the taxes from education, sanitation and public works into the pockets of *caciques*, political underlings and private accounts. The *cacique* system, crushing all independent opposition, provokes no reaction. Barret does as he is told, as do the others. There is none of Ruiz Zorrilla's conviction that revolution is the only realistic possibility (*16*, 367). Blasco Ibáñez appears to have forgotten the training he received at the hands of Ruiz Zorrilla during the Paris exile.

The overall impression is that the peasants are basically good if left alone. Their satisfaction at harvest-time, their pride in their *barracas*, expressed most clearly through Batiste, indicates a vague notion of a peasant Arcadia: man in harmony with nature living the simple life. Vázquez Cey has drawn attention to the Homeric and Biblical quality of many of the descriptions of peasants at work, not least the girls fetching water from the Fuente (94).

> Ni la menor alusión a la modernidad mecánica y muy

apagada la tocante al complejo vivir urbano. Lo actual en *La barraca* no es sino persistencia, eco de costumbres que se adivinan perennes, provenidas de tiempos primordiales*.

Yet, as we have seen, nature is all too often a sinister force and Arcadia gives way to violence.

Junoy's view that the novel "es una pintura valiente de la ignorancia y de las injusticias de abajo" and Dionisio Pérez's comment that the novel treats "el problema de la lucha por la existencia, del derecho al pan y al trabajo" seem near the mark. But for all this idealism, the overall impression is of confusion and ambiguity. If we do feel that "the land should belong to those who till it"† there still remains the feeling expressed by C. Barja. Blasco Ibáñez, he argues, was fascinated by material things :

> el resultado es una impresión de oquedad espiritual, de ausencia de valores ideales, . . . una acusada tosquedad y una esencial falta de sensibilidad y de delicadeza para todo lo que sea problemas del espíritu (5, 395).

J. León Roca's vision of the sickles of the *huerta* raised in the struggle "por la emancipación del arrendador, y un grito de protesta social . . . viril protesta y de clamor humano", (*12*, 21) is too narrow a view. There is no real revolution in the novel. The reaction to capitalist exploitation is mainly passive and pessimistic. Peasant might devour peasant, man is inhuman to man, the innocent suffer; but in the final analysis no remedy is offered. Peasant solidarity is fragile when hunger and privation gnaw and threaten. The very poor have little faith in socialist revolution or utopias when they put at risk the little they have gained. And the capitalists exploit the situation. Revolt in *La barraca* only harms the innocent. The novel may be a cautionary tale to the effect that radical action will bring a worse suffering. After all, the real historical situation is re-arranged. Barret is made the victim of the "huelga de los colonos" whereas Batiste, the hero, is made the victim first of a natural disaster, the drought, and only

---

*A. Vázquez Cey, '*La barraca*, novela mediterránea', *Humanidades* (Argentina), 24 (1934), 306.
†Kiddle, p. xv.

incidentally of the repercussions of revolutionary action.

For all the radicalism of *El Pueblo* the novel may have offered a vicarious experience and an eloquent corrective.

Perhaps the harsh effects of his own actions will be assuaged in the Valencian worker who will identify himself – through self-contemplation – with the protagonists of the *folletines* – *Arroz y tartana, Flor de mayo, La barraca,* – which were very properly written for him by a young *petit bourgeois*, Vicente Blasco Ibáñez (*13*, 126).

Man must attempt to understand his situation, educate himself, adjust to life and work for progress and prosperity within the system. In revolutions those who suffer are those who can ill afford to do so.

As Pepeta recognises Rosario in the barrio de los Pescadores she reflects on the girl's misfortunes and that of her family. "Era natural : donde no hay padre ni madre, la familia termina así" (30). As her thoughts race and Rosario tries to catch up with the news from the *huerta* we learn of the major details of her family's tragedy and the boycott. The conversation is interrupted by the "vozarrón de marimacho" (31) which summons Rosario (Elisa) inside and Pepeta completes her round to return to the *huerta*. Pepeta's reflections on the ruined *barraca* coincide dramatically with the arrival of the cart bearing the hungry and poverty-stricken Borrulls who, to Pepeta's amazement, turn on to the "tierras malditas". Pimentó, the leader of the boycott, is suddenly shaken from his lazy reverie to verify the news that the power of the workers, held for ten years, has just been broken. As a shiver runs through the peasants, nature is indifferent to the news, "seguía risueña y rumorosa". The ingredients of the conflict are prepared. If the Borrulls refuse to leave only tragedy can result. The major characters have been introduced, the pre-history of the boycott and the major theme of the novel sketched out. These essentials are compressed in Pepeta's thoughts about Rosario, their conversation and Pepeta's witness of the family's arrival. The rest of the chapter emphasises the harshness of peasant life.

The second chapter is a flashback that elaborates the tragedy already related. In essence this tragedy is that of the novel itself. A humble peasant, honest and hardworking, is undone by ill-fortune, exploitation and the power of nature and forced from his land. Under the strain he gives way to violence and murder. While nature works through Barret more than Batiste, it nevertheless brutalises them both. Their stories differ when, in revenge on the landowners, a boycott is called. Within a short time the peasants defeat attempts at re-occupation and live in Arcadian peace, the owners "menos exigentes". For ten years a fine balance of power has been maintained. With the arrival of the Borrulls that balance has been disturbed.

Batiste's pre-history, the clearing of the land, Tomba's prophecy and Pimentó's warning form the major features of chapter III. The first explains his readiness to risk staying on after the warning. After years bound to the "círculo de la miseria rural" (56) he has come to a paradise. He will not now sacrifice "lo que era suyo, lo que estaba regado con su sudor y había de dar el pan a toda su familia" (64). The re-building of the *barraca* adds insult to injury, "algo de burla y de reto" (61) and, moreover, stops Tomba's sheep from grazing, "un motivo más de cólera" (60). Pimentó's cowardice prolongs our expectation of the confrontation that terminates the chapter. The gauntlet is finally thrown down and the *huerta* expectations are dashed. Neither the *huertanos* nor Pimentó had reckoned on a man of stronger will. To collective struggle is now added the dimension of personal insult and a contest of individual wills: Batiste versus Pimentó. With the further dimension of Tomba's prophecy, tragedy seems inevitable.

There is, of course, a basic difference between the warnings of Tomba and Pimentó. The latter stands for the *huerta*. The former, above local interests, may be interpreted as the voice of the latent and sinister fatality that permeates the novel. Tomba is the novel's Tiresias. Like Tiresias, the Theban prophet, he is blind but has the gift of prophecy. Like Tiresias he is long-lived and has a staff to guide his steps. His words, spoken "con cierta entonación de hechicero que augura el porvenir o de profeta que husmea la ruina", echo through the story, the clearest expression of some form of transcendental pessimism. Like the prophecy, so the development of each chapter has its own inexorable pattern, a pattern mirrored by the total structure of the novel itself. Now that the exposition is complete we can see the shape of each chapter: a slow passage that presents the setting and the point for discussion, the preparation for the action and a swift rise to a climax and sudden dénouement. In each of the ten parts the theme is the same: the intruders must be forced from the 'blacked' fields. Each chapter, with one exception, ends by emphasising the enmity against the Borrulls, draws attention to the doom that awaits if occupation persists (chapter VII), or explicitly wills an eviction. Only chapter VIII differs. The reason is clear. This chapter initiates the measure of tolerance after Pascualet's death and prepares for chapter IX, the high point of the novel, where the Borrull labours come to fruition. Each chapter, of course, was written as an episode of the *folletín* in *El Pueblo* which would dictate this type of structure.

Chapter IV marks a second collision of wills over Pimentó's calumny and the final defiant taking of the *riego*. At the Tribunal and at the sound of Pimentó's delighted and mocking reenactment of the court decision we witness the first stage of the disintegration of the hero's personality. "¡Rediós! Ahora comprendía él, hombre de paz y padre bondadoso, por qué los hombres matan" (72). Circumstance is beginning to shape his destiny. As the tension slowly increases, he re-lives the experiences of the morning, scolds Roseta and seethes with suppressed rage over his dying crops. This anger grows to a second explosion as the worker hero asserts the rightness of his cause and the waters are freed. He has undergone a further change towards anarchy. "¿Y todo por qué? Por la injusticia de los hombres, porque hay leyes para molestar a los trabajadores honrados . . . Hombre era él capaz de convertirse en ladrón para darles de comer" (78). His environment has shaped the first link in a disastrous chain even though he has won the first round.

The next three chapters shift the interest from the two central combatants to the Borrull family. As Batiste has suffered at the hands of the *huerta*, so do Roseta and Pascualet. Yet their adventures are not self-contained. Chapter IV has already prepared the Roseta-Tonet relationship, for both chapters have a time overlap (93). In spite of her fears and the sense of foreboding that the reader shares, the love-affair flowers. From the simple and matter-of-fact "Perque 't vullc" (91) Tonet becomes a generous dreamer, Roseta the self-conscious *novia*. The line of development appears to be upwards in contrast to the sloping downward line of the combatants. But their sense of well-being is short-lived as the heedless trip to the Fuente demonstrates. Catastrophe is withheld by the descriptive *cuadro*. Only in the final pages is the action suddenly released when Roseta realises that her father is not the only target for attack. The warning that a sense of well-being is deceptive has been given.

Yet chapter VI ironically begins on a note of rustic charm and innocence. The *cuadro* of the schoolroom and the tales of Tomba only give way at the very last to the assault on Pascualet and the infection from the stagnant waters. Again appearances are deceptive. The effects of the outrage on Roseta are carried forward into chapter VII. Indeed the dismissal of Tonet, the resultant effects on Roseta, the death of Morrut and Teresa's "horrible presentimiento" (114) coincide to underline the feeling of "una atmósfera envenenada de odio" that becomes a horrifying reality in the "veneno" Pascualet has taken from the *acequia*. The expected catastrophe is postponed by the dealings of the horse-fair and the high spirits of Batiste on his return with the new horse. But pleasure swiftly slides into despair and grief when a triple burden is placed on the family. The death of a child is the centre of the tragedy. Yet the further effects of brutalisation on the mother (123), and especially on Batiste (125) together with the wounding of the horse, serve to show how near the family had come to repeating Barret's history (128). The echo of Tomba's words and prophecy stress the forces of fatality at work. The lands are indeed "malditas". They who live by the gun will end by it.

The effects of Pascualet's death in chapter VIII re-state the hesitant slant upwards of chapter V when enmity gives way to pity and concern. As if to emphasise the new-found tranquillity there is virtually no action in this chapter, the *albaet* being principally descriptive. Even the conversations underline previous themes: the lack of education, idealised notions of a basically good peasantry, the brutalising effects of social deprivation. The final paragraphs emphasise, however, that this peace is dearly bought, and that nature's power is ever ready to swallow man in its struggle forward. The upward movement is continued in chapter IX, the high point of the novel in terms of human achievement. As the *huerta* basks in sunshine and reaps the bounty of nature, Batiste foolishly forgets the many warnings he has been offered. Lulled into "una impresión de bienestar" (145), he seems heedless of the lessons afforded to Roseta, Pascualet and himself after the horse-fair. Deceptively the "atmósfera envenenada" has disappeared. Batiste "sentía la embriaguez de la tierra" and "desperezándose con voluptuosidad", is "dominado por el bienestar tranquilo de que parecía impregnado el ambiente" (146). At this point Batiste makes his bid 'to belong' and goes to casa de Copa. He is doubly foolish because he not only ignores all the previous warnings but fails to realise the significance of the timing of his visit: San Juan, the time for the rentals and the time of the beginning of Barret's tribulations. He also underestimates the effect of alcohol on himself and Pimentó. Once more, a combination of elements points inexorably to conflict and tragedy. Batiste has failed to perceive the 'reality' of his situation. Pimentó's braggart stories open up the wounds of memory and antagonise a momentarily sympathetic *huerta*. Simply put, "se había roto el encanto". The landowners' fangs are bared once again. For the third time Pimentó and Batiste face one another. This time blood is shed. As Batiste notices the "manchas negruzcas de la sangre ya seca" (161) on the bar-stool before tossing it into the nearby *acequia*, his tragedy nears its *dénouement*. The stains are omens of the blood that is still to be shed.

The final chapter shows the family embattled as never before. Batiste now lives entirely by the law of the gun. "Su hazaña de la taberna había modificado su carácter, antes pacífico y sufrido, despertando en su interior una brutalidad agresora" (164). His character disintegration is complete, the *bête humaine* has emerged under the stresses of circumstance. The chapter has two climaxes, the first preparing the second. The ambush and the chase have all the qualities of the cinema. The swift panning, the camera rapidly cutting in and out, the blurred race along the cane groves are features that ensured Blasco Ibáñez's success with the Hollywood impresarios. Betoret Paris has properly commented that "han sido necesarios los adelantos del arte cinematográfico para llegar al mismo resultado" (9, 279). The major climax is reached when the fires of hell of the fevered dream suddenly become the flames that consume the *barraca*. As they watch their prosperity devoured by the holocaust "con la pasividad de fatalismo" (180) they see their efforts as mere illusions. A traditional image of *desengaño*, the embers of the fire*, underlines the pessimism of the novel.

*See Góngora, *Soledad primera*, ll. 680–686.

What is most remarkable about *La barraca* is its cyclic structure. The novel begins and ends with dawn on a ruined *barraca*. The lands are restored by flames (58) as they are destroyed by flames (177ff). We have already noted the reiteration of the image of hunger "mordiéndoles los talones" which underscores the cyclic structure. We have also noted the extraordinary similarity of the Barret story to that of Batiste. Both are exploited by the family of don Salvador; both struggle with the soil and Batiste feels "lo mismo que el difunto tío Barret, . . . la embriaguez de la tierra" (145). On three occasions the most important likeness is stressed : that of the man who through no fault of his own is forced to leave the land and becomes a killer. As Batiste's personality gradually charts a distinctly downward curve the parallel is forged. After the frustrated attempt to shoot Pimentó in chapter VII Tomba warns him that "acabaría matando tontamente como el pobre Barret" (128). This repeats a warning in chapter III and forms a circle within the greater cycle. Whether Blasco Ibáñez is observing his Naturalist 'experiment' or trying to show how man is heedless of reality, both men break down under the pressures of hunger, incessant toil, exploitation and natural forces. Thus Barret steals water (40) as Batiste does later (79). Their reactions to the soil are identical (40 & 76). Both suffer from the drought, both lose their horses and borrow from the landlords. Both take up the gun in anger. At Pimentó's ultimatum in casa de Copa the situation offers a parallel to Barret and the bailiffs. Even the terms are similar. Barret's "amor de sus amores, eran aquellas tierras" (37) is mirrored by Batiste's "tierras, que eran como la carne de su cuerpo" (159). Both are affected by alcohol when violence breaks out. Barret becomes a beast at the sight of don Salvador who dies a "res degollada". Batiste becomes a beast as he feels "el comezón de homicidio" (168) and Pimentó crawls away "una gran culebra". One tragedy repeats another. On a larger time scale the Moors' eviction centuries before is mirrored by that of Barret. At the arrival of the bailiffs Barret feels "en su interior la ciega bravura del mercader moro que sufre toda clase de ofensas, pero enloquece de furor cuando le tocan su propiedad" (44). Batiste understands too why the Moors wept as they were evicted (145). The news of the arrival of strangers spreads "como

si no hubiesen transcurrido los siglos" (36). Even Nature eternally
repeats itself "engendrando cosecha tras otra", as does the water
"circulando . . . a todas horas" (57). The life of the peasants is an
unbroken daily cycle of work. Batiste is imprisoned "siempre
dentro del círculo de la miseria rural" (56).

The structure and the duplication of events and histories seem
more than coincidental. This motif could be linked with a
number of thought-currents that had begun to emerge at the end
of the nineteenth century. While there is no evidence that Blasco
Ibáñez had read Kierkegaard or Nietzsche* at this time, there
may be an attempt here to render in literary terms their theories
concerning repetition and eternal recurrence subsequently so
influential in the novels of the Generation of 1898. Briefly, the
interpretation of the new ideas was deeply pessimistic and
suggested that man was caught in a cycle of history that repeats
itself in a process of eternal duplication. With none of the joy of
identification with the cosmic forces of expansion, culmination,
decline and rebirth of Nietzsche's Zarathustra, the Valencian's
pessimism is revealed in the hopelessness of a renewal that brings
no progression. As Barret's expulsion mirrors that of the Moors
and Batiste's eviction that of Barret, we see that the continuous
rise and fall of lifetimes is cyclic. Each revolution of that cycle
will repeat the motion of previous revolutions as, paradoxically,
it also destroys itself in anticipation of renewal. Life becomes a
meaningless habit. Man's toil and aspirations come to nothing.
As man labours, blind to the portents, he is mocked by a cosmos
that eternally renews itself without change. This is why, for all
the warnings offered to Batiste and all the parallels with Barret
afforded him, he cannot escape the pattern set. Two steps forward are really one forward and one back.

The ending seems to hover dangerously between the appear-
ance of a genuine compassion for the family as well as for the
peasants (an uneasy position in itself) and (in ironic juxtaposition)

*G. Sobejano's *Nietzsche en España*, Madrid, 1967, quotes no specific reference
to Nietzsche's writings at the time of writing *La barraca*. However, given the
intellectual ethos of Nietzschean ideas in the late '90s described in the introductory
chapters of Sobejano's monograph it seems very unlikely that Blasco Ibáñez
could have remained ignorant of the German's philosophy.

that of a more aesthetic pleasure for its own sake as the author surveys with satisfaction the outcome of his Naturalistic 'experiment' and the 'beauty' of the novel's architecture. The reasons for this confrontation are obscure but such irony is reminiscent of Zola. Even if we know that man is a victim of given environmental and hereditary features, that he is caught in a cycle of history, we might condemn the author of a seemingly radical novel for choosing this moment to bring it up.

Several critics have argued that the novel has epic qualities. Beginning in 1899 with Luis Ruiz Contreras' "hay algo épico en este cruel episodio" the theme is re-echoed by Pitollet's "su acción es de una simplicidad épica" (4, 219). The characters are carried along, heedless of the portents, to a tragic consummation they cannot avoid. An atmosphere of sinister foreboding serves as a backdrop to this trajectory. Kiddle sees the novel as a three-act drama: Act I (chapters 1-3), the Past Tragedy and Opening Conflict; Act II (4-7), The Increasing Conflict; Act III (8-10), The Momentary Peace and Final Disaster*. While dramatic, there is little to suggest an epic quality. First the hero is not of the 'high mimetic mode'† required of epic, and while there is a hint of a transcendental world of sinister power, there is nothing of the epic dimension of the relationship between man and the supernatural.

Rather the novel echoes the pessimism of the early Zola where we see man attempting to rise above his condition to a peak of insecure felicity from which he falls rapidly to the difficulties from which he rose. Such a conical structure (given the circular base) is a common feature of Zola's novels. The banquet scene of *L'Assommoir* marks the high point of Gervaise's fortunes whence she falls to the gutter from which she came. The marriage of Jean and Françoise and the joy at land-tenure in *La Terre* give way quickly to Jean's agony at his wife's death and his decision to leave the region for the army whence he first came. A similar pattern emerges in *Germinal*. Batiste cannot overcome. Man must strive for his daily bread but that striving brings unbidden

---

*Introduction to *La barraca*, New York, 1960, p. xiv.
†Northrop Frye, *Anatomy of Criticism: Four Essays*, Princeton, 1957.

evils (179). Man, a victim (132), bears the burden of "la mala suerte" (56) with "resignación oriental". There is more hopelessness than protest. It is the Zola of pessimistic Naturalism rather than of radical political optimism who seems most influential here.

If, as Kiddle has argued, Batiste's victory is that "it will be harder in the future to unite the community against a newcomer" (xv), that victory is a Pyrrhic one.

This novel has a simple classical story line. Its unwavering rise and fall describes a parabola. The novel may present us with a series of quasi-autonomous *cuadros* but they are subservient to the whole. In the same way there is a rise and fall of the hero, which is not allowed to obscure the central naturalistic theme. Batiste's character never breaks free from the pattern that Blasco Ibáñez has prepared for him. In a way we have a dual vision of the hero. We see him as apparently autonomous, dispassionately observed by the author, making concrete material gains in a situation fraught with difficulty and, temporarily, triumphing over life. But the triumph is short-lived. The seeds of disaster are present from the beginning, invisible to the unreflective Batiste who fails to heed Tomba's prophecy and the obvious portents. Gradually there emerges a pattern that is more significant than the adventures of the hero. Indeed, it cuts across the parabolic line. Each chapter begins with the fresh sally of the Borrull family against life. Each chapter allows them to come to some conclusion concerning their situation. Each chapter ends on their fears and the symptoms of their disintegration, especially marked in the case of Batiste. At the Tribunal (69), at Pimentó's mocking echo of the sentence (72), on the stealing of the *riego* (79), the attack on Pimentó's house (125), casa de Copa (160) and the final "cacería humana" the reader is brought face to face with the gradual breakdown of character. Yet each time the fears and symptoms are superseded or forgotten by the character in the next chapter in spite of the instructive parallels of the rise and fall of Barret. The reader is simultaneously engaged in observing the apparent autonomy and reality of Batiste's struggle while he also witnesses the way in which the author presents the more permanent realities. Batiste's blindness or disregard for those realities is the guarantee of the inevitability of his downfall for it is this very blindness that makes the fiction convincing. Batiste accepts his downfall "con resignación oriental" (180). He never

speaks of the fatality that conspires against him. It is shown to
the reader by the gradual crushing of the individual will, the
obstruction of the family purpose, as each chapter reinforces the
themes of a sinister destiny latent in nature and the power of
the forces of heredity and of social injustice. Only rarely do we
need an authorial intrusion to underscore the point as in the
description of Batiste's pre-history : "La mala suerte le perseguía"
(56). As the hero is progressively brutalised by enmity, hard work
and the everpresent threat of eviction and hunger he relies more
and more on the law of the gun. He is brave but has little understanding of the way men think and react. Indeed, after the clash
of wills with Pimentó, "hasta sentía cierto goce secreto provocán-
dolo, marchando rectamente hacia él" (164). Once "pacífico y
sufrido", he now shows "una brutalidad agresora" (164). His
heedless decision to visit casa de Copa contributes directly to this
pattern of disintegration. His rationalization of the urge to
'belong' is as primitive and clumsy as his behaviour there (148
& 153). As the mass movement reaches a climax of anger and
resentment under the influence of alcohol, Batiste, inebriated too,
reaches without thought for the nearest bar-stool. As for Zola, so
here, alcohol is a convenient artistic device that enables the author
to explain situations beyond the bounds dictated by sober realism
and verisimilitude. But alcohol does not explain the total collapse
of control. In a way Blasco Ibáñez enters into the righteous indignation of this basically good man as an artist identifying himself
with his task. It is a part of the requirements of telling a 'good
story'. Another requirement is that events should be painted on a
broader canvas than a purely deterministic one. While man's
place in the scheme of things can be understood in terms of man
la bête humaine, the subrational instinctive creature, there is also
the aspect, again strikingly portrayed in Zola, of man as self-
conscious.

Blasco Ibáñez, like Zola, "on one level sees man collectively as
identified with the species and finds him steeped in the physical
world. On the other level he sees man as an individual and takes
a wistful glance at the refinements to be found in 'the moral
world', where manifestations of consciousness are fragile wisps of
reality" (*14*, 99). Thus, Batiste, passive and earth-bound, feels

and is aware of loyalty to family and his duty to provide for them when his tenancy is threatened. Just so is Barret prepared to give his blood as much out of a love for his family as for the soil. His refusal to burden them with his economic difficulties bears silent witness to his concern. Even Pimentó becomes submissive in the general guilt over the death of Pascualet. Roseta, while like her father, also represents a hesitant move towards an ideal concep-tion of love in a naturalistic world. This idealism is revealed in the innocence, the timidity and purity of feeling that grows up between her and Tonet. As with the lovers of *Germinal* the "two young lovers . . . stand at the threshold of a world far above the level of mass humanity, and it is altogether conceivable that [the author] lets his secret aspirations with regard to the individual's place in the world be idealistically expressed in his depiction of this relationship" (*14*, 104). The placing of the forcible breaking of the *noviazgo* alongside the deaths of Morrut and Pascualet seems to underline this view. Man feels for his fellows, he is even sentimental over his animals. Yet he is also capable of a sudden descent to primitive savagery in accordance with his Moorish ancestry. Unlike the characters created by other Spanish 'Natur-alist' writers, all those in this novel are depicted as inseparable from the world they inhabit. Nowhere do we have persons who offer anything separate, as representatives either of a more cultured world or of a higher spirituality. Compared with, say, the dualistic world of the novels of Pardo Bazán, Blasco Ibáñez's is a monistic one.

It is on this issue that there is a basic difference of critical opinion. Betoret Paris argues that since the characters are painted from real life they have a credible psychology (*9*, 39-40 & 235). This argument is further elaborated in the *Hispania* essay of 1969. Blasco Ibáñez, he asserts, "posee el arte de crear personajes y sintetizar psicologías colectivas" (101). Pimentó, he asserts, is a perfect example of 'behaviourism' *avant la lettre* in that he is a synthesis of *huertano* attitudes. On the other hand C. Barja seeks "valores de psicología" in vain. "En cuanto a psicología, no pasa de la elemental de las más inmediatas y más ordinarias reacciones. De lo cual resulta que el autor no es novelista de almas ni creador de caracteres" (*5*, 395). "Es el tipo de hombre de acción . . . de

la voluntad terca y enérgica, del aragonés que Blasco Ibáñez lleva
dentro de sí, tipo que va desde *La barraca* . . ." (5, 396). This
view is supported by Angel del Río's *Historia de la literatura
española* (New York, 1963), and more caustically by Torrente
Ballester.

While there are some psychological portrayals they are, in the
main, crude and superficial. Rosario's reaction of shame (30),
don Salvador's exploitation of Barret's submissive nature (40),
Pimentó's bullying, the ritual of the horse-buying, Pepeta's identification with Teresa (132) have a ring of truth and of observed
reality. They do not add up to a penetrating psychological insight.
Rarely do we learn what is actually going on in the minds of the
characters, only the outward manifestation of their feelings. K.
Reding has argued that Blasco Ibáñez "individualizes fewer
characters than Zola"[*]. But the term 'character' begs the question. Are these writers interested in character as the novelistic
presentation of figures who gradually assume their own personality and presence and who, increasingly in nineteenth-century
fiction, take on an autonomous role? Or are they 'attitudes',
vehicles for the ideas of the artist?

In the preface to the second edition of *Thérèse Raquin* (1868),
Zola wrote:

> In *Thérèse Raquin* my aim has been to study temperaments
> and not characters. That is the whole point of the book. I have
> chosen people who are totally dominated by their nerves and
> their passions, lacking in free will, drawn into each action of
> their lives by the inexorable laws of their physical make-up.
> Thérèse and Laurent are human animals, nothing more. I
> have endeavoured to follow, step by step, the dark working of
> the passion of these animals, the compulsion of their instincts
> and the unhingeing of their minds as a result of a nervous
> crisis. The sexual encounters of my hero and heroine are the
> satisfaction of a need; the murder they commit a direct conse-
> quence of their adultery, a consequence they accept just as
> wolves accept the slaughter of sheep. Last, what I have had to
> call their remorse, comes down to a simple organic disorder,

[*]Hispania (U.S.A.), 6 (1923), 368.

the overturning of the nervous system when strained to breaking-point. There is a complete absence of soul, I freely admit, since this is just how I meant it to be.

I trust that by now it will be clear that my object has been primarily a scientific one. When my two characters, Thérèse and Laurent, were created, I amused myself by setting and solving certain problems: I tried to explain the mysterious attraction that is produced between two different temperaments, and I demonstrated the deep-seated convulsions as a sanguine nature is brought into contact with a nervous one. If the novel is read with care, it will be seen that each chapter is the study of a curious psychological case. In a word, I had only one desire: given a highly-sexed man and an unsatisfied woman, to seek for the animal nature in them and isolate that alone, then throw them together in a violent drama and note down with scrupulous attention the sensations and actions of these creatures. I simply applied to two living bodies the analytical methods that surgeons apply to corpses.

The common materialistic cult of environment, heredity and sex in Zola and Blasco Ibáñez as an explanation of human behaviour produces somewhat similar protagonists. If the writer wishes to stress the fatal pressures of environment he will not choose for the demonstration highly individual, independent, dynamic personalities. Rather he must prefer basically weak or unstable people whom the fatality of environment or irresistible nature can easily crush or mould. The naturalist-scientist chose favourable material to work on. Batiste might represent the aspirations of the proletariat in a revolutionary march forward by strength and will alone but he bears within him the genes of *la bête humaine*. Even Zola in the prologue quoted is forced, when faced with the psychological, rather than physiological, problem of remorse, to admit that he has loaded the dice and taken an over-simplified and barely representative case. Indeed, in *Thérèse Raquin*, he so arranges events that "it would have been a miracle if anything other than adultery and murder had been the outcome"*. A close study of Zola's paragraphs quoted above reveals the sham of the 'scientific demonstration' and the

*L. Tancock, Introduction to *Thérèse Raquin*, London, The Folio Society, 1969, p. 9.

patent absurdity of applying empirical experimental criteria to literature. The naturalist experiment is rigged.

Blasco Ibáñez might take the following as data: a forceful, brave, stubborn man emerging from the privations of a four-year drought, the effects of hunger and destitution and a history of failure; a collective consciousness of proletarian solidarity in revolt against years of economic exploitation, a group lacking education and proper political expression. He might place his characters in an environment consisting of a luxuriant and sinister nature. Finally, when the inevitable happens, he might demonstrate with much scientific seriousness that natural instinct coupled with social exploitation and injustice brings about human tragedy. Yet the experiment does not convince. The formula is to arrange some 'tempéraments', add some vague biological and hereditary jargon, deliberately omit the interplay of character and all purely psychological actions, and call the mixture fatality.

While no real 'character' emerges in the novel, the author does break the mask of impersonality to identify with the characters. Indeed, he feels so strongly that he is forced to divide his sympathies when Batiste's breaking of the boycott incurs the animosity of the *huerta*. Perhaps it is don Joaquín who speaks most clearly for the author. He alone recognises their social deprivation, their misery, their parochialism, their lack of education. At times there appears something resembling a moral statement. His comments imply that a lack of tolerance and control, stemming from the lack of education, directly contribute to the deterioration of character and intellect, revealing the beast in man. *La barraca* may be a cautionary tale for radicals and reactionaries alike. To the one, it says that not revolution but education and self-control will help man to progress; to the other, that exploitation, misery, crippling toil, and the numbing effects of alcohol can deprive man of his reason. When the brute is revealed, the uneducated man sets out on a course of action that at first is only destructive of his neighbour. But as his actions overflow the boundaries of the *huerta*, there is the danger that his violence may begin the road to revolution. Given the environmental conditions and a propitious temperament the tragedy will work itself out as inexorably as a Greek drama. Perhaps the name of the hero is symbolic. Batiste is the herald of a new age; he is not the Messiah himself.

8 Stylistic features

The novel has many interesting stylistic features. As we have seen, *La barraca* has much about it that is naturalistic and that discussion need not be reiterated here. While in many ways Naturalist experimentation led to an emphasis on content and a concomitant neglect of form and style, Blasco Ibáñez does not follow the general Naturalist preference for the amorphous form that Zola later transcended. V. A. Chamberlin has shown, for example, that the novel contains "una unidad creadora", through the use of two motifs: "las imágenes animalistas y el uso del color rojo" (*11*, 23). He argues that "desde las primeras páginas el autor presenta la convivencia de hombres y animales e ilustra como comparten ciertas características de cada especie" (*11*, 25). Thus Barret under the sentence of eviction becomes a wild beast and don Salvador his animal victim. The bestial nature of man also lurks in man's psyche as Roseta's dream shows (*11*, 26). The Borrull tribulations are linked to animal imagery, especially in the crescendo passage culminating in the wounding of the horse and the death and burial of Pascualet. The child is presented "balando débilmente" (122); the mother "lanzaba . . . aullidos de fiera enfurecida" (123, repeated at 138); Batiste becomes a "jabalí furioso" (125); the dog takes on a human sympathy (135) and chapter VIII ends with Batiste's sigh, "como el estertor de una bestia herida" (141). The climax of the novel shows an intensification of this imagery, especially during the chase. The colour red, argues Chamberlin, underlines and reinforces the theme of brutality. The glow of the "sol africano" is described at the outset as "enorme oblea roja" (28) which colours the mountains, the city towers, the clouds and the watercourses (28). The church façade at the Tribunal is "rojiza" (65) as is the soil (*passim*) which stains the *acequias* red. Barret's family have coloured the soil with their blood (37) and as Barret's strength fails the land enfolds him "como un sudario rojo" (41). Images of redness underline the ferocity of the scenes of struggle: Barret and

Salvador, the confrontation at the Tribunal, Roseta's struggle at the Fuente and the last two fights, in casa de Copa and the "cacería humana". "Se puede percibir", notes Chamberlin, "su consistencia, y su tremenda fuerza y vitalidad, al desempeñar ellos un recio papel complementario" (*11*, 34). The two images reinforce one another to depict the ferocity and brutality of the atmosphere and the inhabitants of the *huerta*. Chapters IV and V of this study have shown the reasons why Blasco Ibáñez depicted his characters and their environment in this way and how the imagery works. However (as Chamberlin has noted) we should not overlook the fact that, even though there is a strong social message, Blasco Ibáñez also involves us emotionally in our reaction to these two dominant and recurrent images.

One of the main tenets of Naturalist doctrine was impersonality and objectivity. But however hard they tried, the Naturalists could not in practice maintain this degree of scientific objectivity. To put it bluntly, the narrator could not be eliminated from the novel. One of the central problems in the latter half of the nineteenth century was that of reconciling the apparent contradiction between subjectivity and a desire for 'scientific' objectivity. Naturalism, built on the fallacy of dispassionate empirical report, was a triumph only by virtue of the fact that the individual imagination of the artist emerged as it was bound to, to create literature rather than a scientific pamphlet. In *La barraca* we rarely hear the author's voice. A. González Blanco was one of the first critics to notice this essential departure from the omniscient author technique of a Pereda or Galdós (*6*, 605). The problem is resolved by the use of the Zolaesque *style indirect libre*. This enables the author to present his characters without drawing attention to the fact that he is omniscient, either commenting on their thoughts (from outside) or able to read their thoughts and articulate them (from inside). Instead there is no dialogue, or rather, no dialogue in the first person save for the occasional direct interjections in Catalan dialect. Dialogue is rendered as a sort of *oratio obliqua*, a third-person impersonal account of first-person utterance. Such is the technique of Batiste's reply to Pimentó when they first meet (64). At other times speech is rendered as a part of the narrative itself as with the 'conversation

between Pepeta and Rosario (30). It is usually only in moments
of excitement, anger or alarm that any direct speech is used. By
contrast with the dominant 'impersonal relation' this directness
emphasises and underlines the drama of the situation. The reader
is deceived into believing himself in the characters' minds. This
is a trick. He does not see how they think, he watches them react
when faced with given situations.

Pitollet reproduces verbatim Blasco Ibáñez's observations on
the craft of fiction (4, 207-208). Although dictated in 1921, they
are nevertheless illuminating for the study of *La barraca*. For
Blasco Ibáñez, style was "un lugar secundario". "La principal
cualidad del novelista consiste en hacer olvidar su papel de inter-
mediario entre sus lectores y la fábula de su libro." The reader
must forget "que tiene delante de los ojos una historia inventada
por un señor y cree de veras asistir . . . al espectáculo de una acción
que se desarrolla a su vista". Hence, presumably, the manner in
which dialogue is presented. We know what is being said but we
do not see the author pulling the strings to make his puppets say
it.

Yet, for all the claims to the impersonal manner, very often the
adjectives used break the surface objectivity to express some
sympathy or judgement. Two examples, as we have noted, are
the presentations of Barret and don Salvador. The same is equally
true of Pimentó and Batiste when face to face, though, alone,
Pimentó receives a grudging admiration. The use of irony also
betrays the objective presentation. As González Blanco noted,
Blasco Ibáñez uses irony crudely. "La ironía fría y noble . . . no
la conoce Blasco sino en su forma tosca y ruda" (6, 538). Examples
of such lack of a finer touch are to be found in the references to
don Salvador (41 & 57) and the account of Pimentó's 'modesty'
(155). Another intrusion upon objectivity is an evident streak of
sentimentality, a quality praised by *Pigmalión** who admires the
author's 'ternura'. Yet, at times, Blasco Ibáñez's feelings border
on the vulgar. Much of the inimical criticism of the novelist has
made considerable capital of this weakness. Torrente Ballester†

---

*J. M. Meliá, 'Pigmalión', *Blasco Ibáñez, novelista*, Valencia, 1963, pp. 95-96
†Torrente Ballester, *Literatura española contemporánea*, Madrid, 1949, p. 179.

and Blasco Ibáñez's arch-enemy Baroja‡ are outstanding examples. As the *vega* awakens and the power of nature is emphasised in the opening paragraphs of the novel the tone is interrupted by the trite interpolation of human aspirations into the song of the sparrows (26-27). The author also places similar anthropomorphic sentiments in the mind of the cow *La Ròcha* (27-28). The same is true of the sparrows that mock the schoolchildren (100), and the family dog on the death of Pascualet and the entry of the *huertanos* into the *barraca* (135-36). On other occasions there is a feeling of naiveté. Whether the author is writing down to the reader or whether it is unconscious, it nevertheless obtrudes. The picture of the simple life of the Barret girls seems forced with the inclusion of the qualifying "unos ángeles de Dios" (37). It is almost as if the description were spoken by a simple peasant rather than an impersonal observer. Realistic observation is stretched to the limits of parody in the naive account of how the children would visit the stable yet again to make sure the horse was still there (122). The author also employs a series of ready-made clichés that he probably acquired during his apprenticeship under Fernández y González, the historical-serial novelist: the dogs bark only on the arrival of don Salvador "como si se aproximase la muerte" (39), the general description of the usurer as the evident villain and Barret's vision of him as a demon (49). At other times the reader is confronted with all the heavy sentimentality of the worst aspects of nineteenth-century art. The account of the death of Morrut (113) and the vision of angels ascending after Pascualet's death (127 & 129) have all the qualities of an overdone and emasculated bourgeois Romanticism. One is reminded of the exemplary Restoration paintings of Rosales and the early Sorolla, a close friend of the author. Espina's assertion that Blasco Ibáñez "no fue nunca cursi"* is not consistent with the evidence.

Yet while such stylistic features obtrude, on the credit side there are striking images: Barret's "gorro . . . ya no se detenía en sus orejas; aprovechando la creciente delgadez, bajaba hasta los hombros como un fúnebre apagaluz de su existencia" (41).

‡P. Baroja, *Memorias*, Madrid, 1955, especially pp. 428–527.
*A. Espina, 'Ojeada sobre Blasco Ibáñez', *Revista de Occidente*, 58 (1968), 61.

Similarly the shipwreck image applied to the Borrulls (59 & 76); the white *barraca* where the dying Pascualet moans feverishly is already "una sepultura limpia y brillante" (121); the trumpet's "metálica carcajada de la muerte" (140); the sickles "tonsurando los campos" (142).

By means of animal imagery, of images of brutality and symbols of violence and foreboding the author prepares the reader for the inevitable tragedy. In this novel Blasco Ibáñez was approaching the height of his powers, realised in the composition of *Cañas y barro* four years later. After that, unfortunately, as E. Mérimée had predicted†, his over-exuberance and easy impressionism undermined his best qualities. *La barraca* stands as a reminder of that early genius.

†E. Mérimée, 'Blasco Ibáñez et le roman de moeurs provinciales', *Bulletin Hispanique*, 5 (1903), 300.

9 Conclusion

For all Blasco Ibáñez's Republican campaigns, for all the anti-war propaganda of *El Pueblo*, for all the attempts to shame the Valencian public authorities into a greater concern for the quality of life of the inhabitants of the *provincia*, the overall effect of *La barraca* seems to be of a pervasive uneasiness concerning the potential for human progress. While Blasco Ibáñez the author of *La barraca* seems less certain about revolutionary zeal, we find Blasco Ibáñez the Republican deputy and editor of a radical newspaper arguing for progress through direct political action. How do we explain this apparent contradiction? Perhaps the reflective writer was a different animal from the figurehead of the Liga Valenciana, the man who was forced by outside pressures to behave and speak publicly in a given way. At all events the novel is concerned with less clear-cut issues, with more diffuse factors that make up the substance of the tragedy of the human condition. In many ways *La barraca* is open-ended. It has been praised by Sebastià, Betoret Paris and León Roca as a "protesta social". Torrente Ballester has roundly condemned the author as "un típico burgués de izquierdas". These contrasting views suggest that in Spain, at least, the novel has been interpreted as a challenge to the accepted social order. One might say that the 'dos bandos' saw Blasco Ibáñez as a radical voice who questioned the basic assumptions that governed certain areas of social and political influence (notably the problem of land-tenure) and the control of legal authority. Restoration politics have been generally criticised by modern historians for being 'parliamentarian' in that for all the political crises (which prompted Galdós' coining of the term *crisología*), there was little social change. The *turno pacífico* was basically resistant to social change since it represented a wide-spread attitude that uncritically respected received ideas and feared for vested interests. The *huertanos* are seen as the symbol of a growing liberal consciousness that seems ready to overturn the socio-political *status quo*.Yet an interpretation of the conflict along these lines seems to widen the differences between the classes, between political viewpoints, so that the end of the novel suggests that no fruitful dialogue is possible, no concessions can be made. The *huertanos* seem as socially prejudiced and blind to the realities of life as the bourgeoisie.

On the other hand there are more cogent reasons for supposing that the author was less partisan than the leader columns of *El Pueblo* would suggest. The novels of Zola and the Naturalists would have indicated that there are ways of perceiving reality other than along simple political battle-lines. The naturalist technique of experiment would have led Blasco Ibáñez to consider a wider range of determining factors. Indeed, the author adopts virtually the full range of naturalistic possibilities: the power of nature, the power of social pressures as well as the human 'experiment', Batiste, who is shaped and finally crushed by these forces. The cyclic structure, the repetitions alongside the deterministic view seem to indicate a pessimistic vision of the world, a world where progress and revolution are doomed to failure if not actually beyond the reach of the underdog. It may be that man is not strong enough to struggle forward, for all his pretensions to a belief in progress. This implies a strictly determined view of the most negative kind. The 'experiment' could have taught him, however, that even determinism can mislead in that while the elements that make up the fate of the Borrulls are seemingly unchangeable, the outcome could have been other than it was. For all the shaping factors that Batiste suffers he is basically an honest man who manifests a strong sense of love and duty, a sense of right and wrong. Batiste and Barret rely not on their basic feeling for justice, nor even on their ability to discriminate between right and wrong actions when under pressure. They put their trust in their strength and the gun. As the tragedy unfolds we see the folly of such a reaction. Is this a part of the lesson? Force of arms provides a temporary solution, it does not tackle the root causes of the conflict. Perhaps Blasco Ibáñez is arguing that Restoration politics had concerned itself with maintaining law and order by force, the Civil Guard and rigged elections. In the same way the radical left would change the system by revolt. The proper role of government is to analyse the social ills and make the necessary changes that will cure them. Without such change at the grass-roots, class divisions and hatreds will continue to boil over to precipitate human tragedy. While the ruling élite is inhuman to the workers, with the enmity unleashed on Batiste, man is also inhuman to man. The novel offers a moral as well as a social message. In fact, as we have seen, that lesson was grasped by the earliest critic of the novel. *La barraca*, noted Junoy, "es decirle (al *huertano*) . . . cuán mal obra martirizando de hecho y de palabra". Radicalism without revolution.

If we criticize this pessimistic view of the world it must be, in the final analysis, on grounds of literary incoherence. Blasco Ibáñez seems to promise us one thing and give us another. He seems to overlook the implications of the naturalist method. To many commentators there remains at the end of the novel a feeling of hope, a protest that promises social progress, and yet we are given fatality. If he argues that man should not strive for revolution but work within the system, we are furnished with the evidence for despair. At the root of these confusions is the very choice of the *huertanos* as the bearers of his meaning. The *huerta* as a collective is a house divided against itself; Batiste is at odds with his fellow peasants. They are a perfect instrument for demonstrating the naturalistic vision of forces of nature and heredity, and a convenient symbol for an attack on Restoration social structures from a liberal viewpoint. Yet for all the completeness of this naturalist experiment it refused to serve him exactly as he had hoped. When he attempted constructive criticism of the social order and of the problems of land-tenure it tended to produce what looks like a remote world of indifference, greed, self-interest and corruption in which no progress could be hoped for. If he introduced positive ideas they did not match the human raw material. Humanity is too weak. Batiste's pre-determined weaknesses and the effects of his environment do not make for a hero that would incarnate revolutionary idealism and the science of progress. For all his goodness, Batiste lacks the dynamism to put such ideas into practice. Thus the novelist is driven to try to redress the balance by interpolating fragments that hint at vestiges of goodness, love and faith within the human brute that is the *huertano*. So we admire and believe in Batiste's regard for and sense of duty to his family, we sympathise with the lovers. But we are shown no systematic or dynamic way that these features can be propagated.

It may be that Blasco Ibáñez felt, like many others in the nineteenth century, including Zola, that science and education brought no certain comfort. Belief in the sciences may offer a way forward from ignorance, superstition and tyranny; yet science also seemed to many to deny man's freedom to initiate the progress he sought. With the collapse of a belief in scientific progress all that is left in life is that mankind inhabits a world made up of cruelty, hunger, injustice and inhumanity. In such a world we can only feel sympathy and attempt to understand and come to terms with reality. Herein lies the real value of the novel for all its faults and apparent disappointments. *La barraca* shows how humanity fails to heed eloquent portents. This is the tragedy of the human condition. Man needs to banish ignorance, learn to know himself, be tolerant of others' interests, discover charity. Batiste is only the prophet of the new age that Gabriel Luna, the hero of *La catedral* (1903), is, more crudely and less convincingly, to usher in. The novelist discusses social problems and interprets them but gives no clear-cut solutions. We may object on moral grounds that the picture of mankind caught in the grip of inexorable transcendent forces, and the ultimately complacent depiction of radical ideas foundering in a determined situation are not edifying subjects for literature. It may be, however, that the author is more concerned with the human being at the centre and his 'reality' than the apparent naturalistic presentation would suggest. If man is so enmeshed he should strive to adjust. Man is blind to the realities that the author can perceive. Thus we as readers become aware of those realities and understand the human condition. As Yeats observed in the last letter he wrote, "Man can embody truth but he cannot know it". Reality is not knowable. If aggressively pursued, reality recedes and no solutions or lessons emerge. Only when invoked will it advance and manifest itself in all its contradictory and multivalent aspects. Man embodies truth in art. *La barraca*, then, is a kind of knowing; not an abstract or a scientific enquiry but an act of affirmation of the 'truth' perceived by the artist. He has achieved a more subtle and more satisfactory synthesis between the crude abstractions of 'reality' and 'imagination', and 'objective detachment' and 'subjective sympathy'.

For all the pessimism of the novel there remains that strange inarticulate feeling of idealism that commentators have over-emphasised. Man has an unrealised potential for goodness. As idealism gradually began to gain the initiative against materialism in the 1890s a significant step forward was made. From bald assertion and cold experiment there emerges a movement towards patient understanding and sympathy for the human condition. As William Sharp observed in *The Academy* in 1890:

> The true artist, no doubt, is he who is neither a realist nor a romanticist, but in whose work is observable the shaping power of the higher qualities of the methods of genuine realism and the higher qualities of the methods of genuine romance.

It is the near-realisation of this synthesis that makes *La barraca* a remarkable novel.

Bibliographical note

Editions

The most readily available edition of *La barraca* is that of G. J. G. Cheyne: Vicente Blasco Ibáñez, *La barraca* (Harrap, London, 1964), 236 pp. with introduction, notes and vocabulary. *La barraca* is also published in Vol. 6 of the *Obras completas*, Prometeo, Valencia, and Vol. 1 of the *Obras completas*, Aguilar, Madrid, 1946.

Biography

1 Gascó Contell, Emilio. *Genio y figura de Vicente Blasco Ibáñez* (Madrid, 1921). Reprinted 1957 and 1967. The fullest biography of the novelist. Gascó Contell was Blasco Ibáñez's secretary.
2 Gimeno, Juli Just. *Blasco Ibáñez i València* (Valencia, 1931). In Catalan, and a valuable corrective to some of the details given by a gullible Gascó Contell.
3 Martínez de la Riva, Ramón. *Blasco Ibáñez, su vida, su obra, su muerte, sus mejores páginas* (Madrid, 1929). A derivative study more journalistic than scholarly. Reproduces his correspondence with the author.
4 Pitollet, Camille. *V. Blasco Ibáñez, sus novelas y la novela de su vida* (Valencia, 1922?). Well-documented but over-praising biography. Thin on the critical side.

General Studies

5 Barja, César. *Libros y autores modernos* (Los Angeles, 1933). The section on Blasco Ibáñez, while somewhat dated, is still refreshing in its penetration and refusal to idolise.
6 González Blanco, Andrés. *Historia de la novela en España desde el romanticismo a nuestros días* (Madrid, 1909). Charts Blasco Ibáñez's place in the history of the novel and recognises his Naturalist heritage.
7 León Roca, José Luis. *Vicente Blasco Ibáñez* (Valencia, 1967). The fullest study of the novelist and his writings. Includes valuable information on the social background to *La barraca* [See No. 12] and an extensive bibliography.
8 Ribelles Pérez, Vicente. *Vicente Blasco Ibáñez* (Madrid, 1967). A useful introduction that bears an official imprimatur from the Ministerio de Información y Turismo.

Critical Studies

9 Betoret Paris, Eduardo. *El costumbrismo en la obra de Blasco Ibáñez* (Valencia, 1958). Documents the 'realism' and authenticates the 'costumbres' of the Valencian novels.
10 Blanco Aguinaga, Carlos. *Juventud del '98* (Madrid, 1970). Has a chapter on the socio-political bias of the novels, especially *La bodega*. The introductory commentary is excellent.

11 Chamberlin, Vernon. 'Las imágenes animalistas y el color rojo en *La barraca*', *Duquesne Hispanic Review*, 6 (1967), 23–36. One of the few detailed studies of a stylistic aspect of the novel.

12 León Roca, José Luis. 'Como escribió Blasco Ibáñez *La barraca*', *Les Langues Néo-Latines*, 180 (1967), 1–22. An extract from the larger study (No. 7) that uncovers the historical events that may have provided the story for the novel.

13 Sebastià, Enric. *València en les novel·les de Blasco Ibáñez* (Valencia, 1966). An important study in Catalan applying Arnold Hauser's theories concerning the interaction of society and art to the socio-economic background of the Valencian novels.

Comparative Studies

14 Eoff, Sherman H. *The Modern Spanish Novel* (New York, 1961). An essay compares the common philosophical background of Zola's *Germinal* and *Cañas y barro*. A very suggestive and penetrating study that provides some useful pointers to the interpretation of *La barraca*. Highly recommended.

15 Pérez de la Dehesa, Rafael. 'Zola y la literatura española finisecular', *Hispanic Review*, 39 (1971), 49–69. A masterly study of the importance, for Spanish liberals, of Zola as a social and political thinker.

Historical Background

16 Carr, Raymond. *Spain 1808–1939* (Oxford, 1966). A scholarly and clearly presented account of the historical background to the novel.

17 Giner, Salvador. *Continuity and Change: The Social Stratification of Spain* (University of Reading Occasional Publication No. 1, 1968). A first-rate concise synthesis of some of the chief characteristics and trends in the stratification of modern Spanish society.